THE coffee
cookbook

THE
coffee
cookbook

OVER 70 IRRESISTIBLE RECIPES FEATURING COFFEE IN DESSERTS AND CAKES

CATHERINE ATKINSON

southwater

This edition is published by Southwater

Southwater is an imprint of
Anness Publishing Limited
Hermes House
88–89 Blackfriars Road
London SE1 8HA
tel. 020 7401 2077
fax 020 7633 9499

Distributed in the UK by
The Manning Partnership
251–253 London Road East
Batheaston
Bath BA1 7RL
tel. 01225 852 727
fax 01225 852 852

Distributed in the USA by
Anness Publishing Inc.
27 West 20th Street
Suite 504
New York, NY 10011
tel. 212 807 6739
fax 212 807 6813

Distributed in Australia by
Sandstone Publishing
Unit 1, 360 Norton Street
Leichhardt
New South Wales 2040
tel. 02 9560 7888
fax 02 9560 7488

1 3 5 7 9 10 8 6 4 2

Publisher: Joanna Lorenz
Editor: Finny Fox-Davies
Designer: Ian Hunt
Photography: William Lingwood
Home Economy: Carol Tennant
Styling: Helen Trent
Editorial Reader: Joy Wotton
Production Controller: Don Campaniello

Previously published as part of a larger compendium, *The World Encyclopedia of Coffee*

Contents

INTRODUCTION

THIS BOOK CONTAINS OVER 70 RECIPES PRESENTED IN A BEAUTIFULLY ILLUSTRATED STEP-BY-STEP FORMAT. ALL THE CLASSIC COFFEE RECIPES ARE INCLUDED, SUCH AS TIRAMISU, COFFEE COEURS À LA CRÈME, MOCHA SPONGE CAKE AND CAPPUCCINO TORTE. THERE ARE ALSO RECIPES FOR ALL OCCASIONS, FROM FRUIT AND FROZEN DESSERTS, SUMPTUOUS TORTES, RICH PIES AND PASTRIES AND IRRESISTIBLE COOKIES AND BREADS. ALL OF THE RECIPES DEMONSTRATE JUST HOW VERSATILE AN INGREDIENT COFFEE IS; IT COMBINES EFFORTLESSLY WITH SO MANY OTHER FLAVORS, SUCH AS ALCOHOL, FRUIT, CHOCOLATE AND CREAM. ALWAYS USE GOOD-QUALITY COFFEE, AND EXPERIMENTING WITH COFFEES FROM AROUND THE WORLD WILL MAKE EACH DISH A DELICIOUS CULINARY ADVENTURE.

HOT AND COLD CREAM DESSERTS

Smooth creamy custards form the base of many cold desserts, such as Coffee Crème Caramel and Petits Pots de Cappuccino, as well as hot ones such as Apricot Panettone Custard. Served in tall elegant glasses, light airy mousses feature frequently among the most memorable desserts. Many are also blissfully simple; such as Coffee Cardamom Zabaglione and Chocolate and Espresso Mousse.

CLASSIC COFFEE CRÈME CARAMEL

THESE LIGHTLY SET COFFEE CUSTARDS ARE SERVED IN A POOL OF CARAMEL SAUCE. FOR A RICHER
FLAVOR, MAKE THEM WITH HALF LIGHT CREAM, HALF MILK.

SERVES SIX

INGREDIENTS
   2½ cups milk
   3 tablespoons ground coffee
   ¼ cup sugar
   4 eggs
   4 egg yolks
   spun sugar, to decorate (optional)
For the caramel sauce
   ¾ cup sugar
   ¼ cup water

1 Preheat the oven to 325°F. To make
the caramel sauce, gently heat the
sugar in a small heavy pan with the
water, until the sugar has dissolved.
Bring to a boil and boil rapidly until
the syrup turns a rich golden brown.

5 Put the ramekins in a roasting pan
and pour in enough hot water to come
two-thirds of the way up the sides of the
dishes. Bake for 30–35 minutes or until
just set. Test by gently shaking one of
the custards; it should wobble like jelly.
Remove the custards from the hot water
and allow to cool.

6 Chill the coffee custards for at least
3 hours. To turn out, carefully loosen
the sides with a metal spatula, then
invert onto serving plates. Decorate
with spun sugar, if using.

COOK'S TIP
To make spun sugar, gently heat scant
½ cup sugar, 1 teaspoon light corn syrup
and 2 tablespoons water in a heavy pan
until the sugar dissolves. Boil the syrup
to 325°F, then briefly dip the base of
the pan into cold water. Put a sheet of
waxed paper on the work surface to
protect it. Holding two forks together,
dip them into the syrup and flick them
rapidly back and forth over an oiled
rolling pin. Store in an airtight container
until ready to use.

2 Quickly and carefully, pour the hot
syrup into six warmed ⅔-cup ramekins.

3 To make the coffee custard, heat the
milk until almost boiling. Pour over the
ground coffee and allow to infuse for
about 5 minutes. Strain through a fine
strainer into a pitcher.

4 In a bowl, whisk the sugar, eggs and
yolks until light and creamy. Whisk the
coffee-flavored milk into the egg
mixture. Pour into the ramekins.

TIRAMISU

THE NAME OF THIS CLASSIC DESSERT TRANSLATES AS "PICK ME UP", WHICH IS SAID TO DERIVE FROM THE FACT THAT IT IS SO GOOD THAT IT LITERALLY MAKES YOU SWOON WHEN YOU EAT IT.

SERVES FOUR

INGREDIENTS

   1 cup mascarpone
   ¼ cup confectioners' sugar, sifted
   ⅔ cup strong brewed coffee, chilled
   1¼ cups heavy cream
   3 tablespoons coffee liqueur such as
     Tia Maria or Kahlúa
   4 ounces ladyfingers
   2 ounces bittersweet or semisweet
     chocolate, coarsely grated
  unsweetened cocoa powder,
     for dusting

1 Lightly grease and line a 2-pound loaf pan with plastic wrap. Put the mascarpone and confectioners' sugar in a large bowl and beat for 1 minute. Stir in 2 tablespoons of the chilled coffee. Mix thoroughly.

2 Whip the cream with 1 tablespoon of the liqueur until it forms soft peaks. Stir a spoonful into the mascarpone mixture, then fold in the rest. Spoon half the mascarpone mixture into the loaf pan and smooth the top.

3 Put the remaining strong brewed coffee and liqueur in a shallow dish just wider than the ladyfingers. Using half the ladyfingers, dip one side of each ladyfinger into the coffee mixture, then arrange on top of the mascarpone mixture in a single layer.

4 Spoon the rest of the mascarpone mixture over the ladyfinger layer and smooth the top.

5 Dip the remaining ladyfingers in the coffee mixture, and arrange on top. Drizzle any remaining coffee mixture over the top. Cover the dish with plastic wrap and chill for at least 4 hours. Carefully turn the tiramisu out of the loaf pan and sprinkle with grated chocolate and cocoa powder; serve cut into slices.

COOK'S TIP
Mascarpone is a silky-textured, soft, thick cream cheese from Italy, now widely available in supermarkets.

COFFEE CARDAMOM ZABAGLIONE

THIS WARM ITALIAN DESSERT IS USUALLY MADE WITH ITALIAN MARSALA WINE. IN THIS UNUSUAL RECIPE COFFEE LIQUEUR IS USED ALONG WITH FRESHLY CRUSHED CARDAMOM.

SERVES FOUR

INGREDIENTS
  4 cardamom pods
  8 egg yolks
  ¼ cup superfine sugar
  2 tablespoons strong brewed coffee
  ¼ cup coffee liqueur such as Tia
    Maria or Kahlúa
  a few crushed roasted coffee beans,
    to decorate

1 Peel the pale green outer husks off the cardamom pods and remove the black seeds. Crush these to a fine powder using a mortar and pestle.

2 Put the egg yolks, superfine sugar and crushed cardamom seeds in a large bowl and beat with an electric hand beater for 1–2 minutes or until the mixture is pale and creamy.

3 Gradually beat the coffee and the liqueur into the egg yolk mixture.

4 Place the bowl over a saucepan of almost-boiling water and continue beating for about 10 minutes.

5 Continue beating until the mixture is very thick and fluffy and has doubled in volume, making sure the water doesn't boil—if it does, the mixture will curdle. Remove the bowl from heat and carefully pour the zabaglione into four warmed glasses or dishes. Sprinkle with a few crushed roasted coffee beans and serve immediately.

COOK'S TIP
Cardamom is a fragrant spice from northern India. It may be bought ground, but freshly crushed cardamom is much sweeter.

PETITS POTS DE CAPPUCCINO

THESE VERY RICH COFFEE CUSTARDS, WITH A CREAM TOPPING AND A LIGHT DUSTING OF COCOA POWDER, LOOK WONDERFUL PRESENTED IN FINE CHINA COFFEE CUPS.

SERVES SIX TO EIGHT

INGREDIENTS
1 cup roasted coffee beans
1¼ cups milk
1¼ cups light cream
1 whole egg
4 egg yolks
¼ cup sugar
½ teaspoon vanilla extract
For the topping
½ cup whipping cream
3 tablespoons ice water
2 teaspoons unsweetened
cocoa powder

1 Preheat the oven to 325°F. Put the roasted coffee beans in a saucepan over low heat for about 3 minutes, shaking the pan frequently.

2 Pour the milk and cream over the beans. Heat until almost boiling; cover and allow to infuse for 30 minutes.

3 Whisk the egg, the egg yolks, sugar and vanilla together. Return the milk to boiling and pour through a strainer onto the egg mixture. Discard the beans.

4 Pour the mixture into eight 5-tablespoon coffee cups or six ½-cup ramekins. Cover each with a small piece of tinfoil.

5 Put in a roasting pan with hot water reaching about two-thirds of the way up the sides of the dishes. Bake them for 30–35 minutes or until lightly set. Let cool. Chill in the refrigerator for at least 2 hours.

6 Whisk the whipping cream and ice water until thick and frothy and spoon on top of the custards. Dust with the cocoa powder before serving.

COOK'S TIPS
These petits pots may also be served warm, topped with a spoonful of whipped cream. Serve immediately, with the whipped cream just starting to melt.

COFFEE AND BRANDY SYLLABUB

THIS HEAVENLY DESSERT COULDN'T BE EASIER—A FROTH OF WHIPPED COFFEE AND BRANDY CREAM TOPS JUICY GRAPES. CRISP COOKIES MAKE A DELICIOUS CONTRAST.

SERVES SIX

INGREDIENTS

6 tablespoons light brown sugar
finely grated zest of ½ orange
½ cup brandy
½ cup cold strong brewed coffee
1⅔ cups heavy cream
8 ounces white seedless grapes
sugared grapes, to decorate
crisp cookies, to serve

COOK'S TIP

For sugared grapes, wash and dry the fruit, then snip into small clusters. Use a fine brush to paint lightly beaten egg white evenly onto the grapes, then dust with superfine sugar. Shake off excess sugar and allow to dry before using.

1 Put the brown sugar, orange zest and brandy into a small bowl. Stir well, then cover with plastic wrap and let stand for 1 hour.

2 Strain the mixture through a fine strainer into a clean bowl. Stir in the coffee. Slowly pour in the cream, whisking constantly.

3 Continue whisking for 3–4 minutes, until the mixture thickens enough to stand in soft peaks.

4 Divide the grapes between the glasses. Pour or spoon the syllabub over the grapes. Chill in the refrigerator for 1 hour. Decorate the glasses with clusters of sugared grapes and serve with crisp cookies.

COFFEE JELLIES

SERVE THESE SPARKLING COFFEE JELLIES AS A LIGHT AND REFRESHING END TO A RICH MEAL.

SERVES FOUR

INGREDIENTS

¼ cup powdered gelatin
5 tablespoons cold water
2½ cups very hot strong brewed coffee
3 tablespoons sugar
For the bay cream
1¼ cups whipping cream
1 tablespoon bay-scented sugar
fresh bay leaves, to decorate

VARIATION

For a creamy version of these jellies, make the coffee with hot milk and serve with fresh fruit instead of bay cream.

COOK'S TIP

To make bay-scented sugar, add 2–3 dried bay leaves to sugar. Set aside for at least a week before using.

1 To make the jellies, sprinkle the gelatin over the cold water. Allow to soak for 2–3 minutes. Add to the hot strong brewed coffee with the sugar and stir to dissolve.

2 Allow the coffee to cool, then pour into four ⅔-cup metal molds. Chill in the refrigerator for 3 hours or until set.

3 To make the bay cream, lightly whisk the cream and bay-scented sugar until very soft peaks form. Spoon into a serving bowl.

4 To serve, dip the molds in a bowl of hot water for a few seconds, then invert onto individual serving plates. Serve with the bay cream and decorate with fresh bay leaves.

COFFEE COEURS À LA CRÈME

THESE PRETTY HEART-SHAPED CREAMS, SPECKLED WITH ESPRESSO-ROASTED COFFEE BEANS, ARE SERVED WITH A FRESH FRUIT SAUCE. USE WILD STRAWBERRIES, IF AVAILABLE, FOR THEIR WONDERFUL AROMA.

SERVES SIX

INGREDIENTS
  generous ¼ cup espresso-roasted
    coffee beans
  1 cup ricotta or cottage cheese
  1¼ cups crème fraîche
  2 tablespoons superfine sugar
  finely grated zest of ½ orange
  2 egg whites
For the red berry coulis
  1 cup raspberries
  2 tablespoons confectioners' sugar,
    sifted
  ⅔ cup small strawberries, (or wild
    ones, if available), halved

1 Preheat the oven to 350°F. Evenly spread the espresso-roasted coffee beans onto a baking sheet and toast for about 10 minutes. Allow to cool, then put in a large plastic bag and crush into tiny pieces with a rolling pin.

2 Thoroughly rinse 12 pieces of muslin in cold water and squeeze dry. Use to line six coeur à la crème molds with a double layer, allowing the muslin to hang the over edges.

3 Press the ricotta or cottage cheese through a fine strainer into a bowl. Stir the crème fraîche, sugar, orange zest and crushed roasted coffee beans together. Add to the cheese and mix well.

4 Whisk the egg whites until stiff and fold into the mixture. Spoon into the prepared molds, then bring the muslin up and over the filling. Let stand in the refrigerator overnight to drain and chill.

5 To make the red berry coulis, put the raspberries and confectioners' sugar in a food processor and blend until smooth. Push through a fine strainer to remove the seeds. Stir in the strawberries. Chill until ready to serve.

6 Unmold the hearts onto individual serving plates and carefully remove the muslin. Spoon the red berry coulis over before serving.

COOK'S TIP
Muslin has a fine weave, which allows the liquid from the cheese to drain through. If you don't have any muslin, use cheesecloth instead.

CHILLED CHOCOLATE AND ESPRESSO MOUSSE

HEADY, AROMATIC ESPRESSO COFFEE ADDS A DISTINCTIVE FLAVOR TO THIS SMOOTH, RICH MOUSSE.
SERVE IT IN STYLISH CHOCOLATE CUPS FOR A SPECIAL OCCASION.

SERVES FOUR

INGREDIENTS

    8 ounces semisweet chocolate
    3 tablespoons brewed espresso
    2 tablespoons unsalted butter
    4 eggs, separated
    sprigs of fresh mint,
      to decorate (optional)
    mascarpone or whipped cream,
      to serve (optional)
For the chocolate cups
    8 ounces semisweet chocolate

1 For each chocolate cup, cut a double thickness 6-inch square of tinfoil. Mold it around a small orange, leaving the edges and corners loose to make a cup shape. Remove the orange and press the bottom of the tinfoil cup gently on a surface to make a flat base. Repeat to make four tinfoil cups.

2 Break the semisweet chocolate into small pieces and place in a bowl set over a pan of very hot water. Stir occasionally until the chocolate has melted.

3 Spoon the chocolate into the tinfoil cups, spreading it up the sides with the back of a spoon to give a ragged edge. Refrigerate for 30 minutes or until set hard. Gently peel off the tinfoil, starting at the top edge.

4 To make the chocolate mousse, put the semisweet chocolate and brewed espresso into a bowl set over a pan of hot water and melt as before. When it is smooth and liquid, add the unsalted butter, a little at a time. Remove the pan from heat, then stir in the egg yolks.

5 Whisk the egg whites in a bowl until stiff, but not dry, then fold them into the chocolate mixture. Pour into a bowl and refrigerate for at least 3 hours.

6 To serve, scoop the chilled mousse into the chocolate cups. Add a scoop of mascarpone or whipped cream and decorate with a sprig of fresh mint, if desired.

APRICOT PANETTONE CUSTARD

SLICES OF LIGHT-TEXTURED PANETTONE ARE LAYERED WITH DRIED APRICOTS AND COOKED IN A CREAMY COFFEE CUSTARD FOR A SATISFYINGLY WARMING DESSERT.

SERVES FOUR

INGREDIENTS

4 tablespoons unsalted
   butter, softened
½-inch thick slices (about 14-ounces)
   panettone containing candied fruit
¾ cup dried apricots, chopped
1⅔ cups milk
1 cup heavy cream
4 tablespoons mild-flavored
   ground coffee
½ cup sugar
3 eggs
2 tablespoons light brown sugar
heavy cream or crème fraîche,
   to serve

1 Preheat the oven to 325°F. Brush an 8-cup oval baking dish with 1 tablespoon of the butter. Spread the panettone with the remaining butter and arrange in the baking dish. Cut to fit and sprinkle the apricots among and over the layers.

2 Pour the milk and cream into a pan and heat until almost boiling. Pour the milk mixture over the coffee and allow to infuse for 10 minutes. Strain through a fine strainer, discarding the coffee grounds.

3 Lightly beat the sugar and eggs together, then whisk in the warm coffee-flavored milk. Slowly pour the mixture over the panettone. Allow to soak for 15 minutes.

4 Sprinkle the top of the custard with light brown sugar and place the dish in a large roasting pan. Pour in enough boiling water to come halfway up the sides of the baking dish.

5 Bake for 40–45 minutes, until the top is golden and crusty, but the middle still soft and moist. Remove from the oven, but let the dish sit in hot water for 10 minutes. Serve warm with heavy cream or crème fraîche.

COOK'S TIP
This recipe works equally well with plain or chocolate-flavored panettone.

SYRUPY COFFEE *and* GINGER PUDDING

THIS COFFEE-CAPPED FEATHER-LIGHT DESSERT IS MADE WITH BREAD CRUMBS AND GROUND ALMONDS.
SERVE WITH CREAMY CUSTARD OR SCOOPS OF VANILLA ICE CREAM.

SERVES FOUR

INGREDIENTS

2 tablespoons light brown sugar
2 tablespoons crystallized ginger,
    chopped
2 tablespoons mild-flavored
    ground coffee
5 tablespoons crystallized ginger
    syrup (from a jar of crystallized
    ginger)
generous ½ cup sugar
3 eggs, separated
¼ cup all-purpose flour
1 teaspoon ground ginger
generous 1 cup fresh
    white bread crumbs
¼ cup ground almonds

1 Preheat the oven to 350°F. Grease
and line the base of a 3-cup pudding
bowl, then sprinkle in the light brown
sugar and chopped ginger.

2 Put the ground coffee in a small bowl.
Heat the ginger syrup until almost
boiling; pour into the coffee. Stir well and
set aside for 4 minutes. Pour through a
fine strainer into the pudding bowl.

3 Beat half the sugar and egg yolks
until light and fluffy. Sift the flour and
ground ginger together and fold into the
egg mixture with the bread crumbs and
ground almonds.

4 Whisk the egg whites until stiff, then
gradually whisk in the remaining sugar.
Fold into the mixture, half at a time.
Spoon into the pudding bowl and
smooth the top.

5 Cover the bowl with a piece of
pleated greased waxed paper and
secure with string. Bake for 40 minutes,
or until the sponge is firm to the touch.
Turn out and serve immediately.

COOK'S TIP
This pudding can also be baked in
a 3¾-cup loaf pan and served
thickly sliced.

SOUFFLÉS
AND
MERINGUES

Fluffy soufflés that rise to the occasion and melt-in-your-mouth meringues—these are coffee desserts to tempt your eye and your palate. The basic ingredients for meringues couldn't be simpler—just egg whites and sugar, to which coffee lends a sophisticated touch. For the perfect finish to a meal, try spicy Floating Islands or the tropical taste of Mango and Coffee Meringue Roll.

CHILLED COFFEE AND PRALINE SOUFFLÉ

A SMOOTH COFFEE SOUFFLÉ WITH A CRUSHED PRALINE TOPPING THAT IS SPECTACULAR AND EASY.

SERVES SIX

INGREDIENTS
¾ cup sugar
5 tablespoons water
generous 1 cup blanched almonds,
plus extra, for decoration
½ cup strong brewed hazelnut-
flavored coffee
1 tablespoon powdered gelatin
3 eggs, separated
scant ½ cup light brown sugar
1 tablespoon coffee liqueur, such as
Tia Maria or Kahlúa
⅔ cup heavy cream
about ⅔ cup heavy cream, for
decoration (optional)

1 Cut a paper collar from a double layer of waxed paper, 2 inches deeper than a 3¾-cup soufflé dish. Wrap around the dish and tie in place with string. Refrigerate.

2 Oil a baking sheet. Put the sugar in a small heavy pan with the water and heat gently until the sugar dissolves. Boil rapidly until the syrup becomes pale golden. Add the almonds and boil until dark golden.

3 Pour the mixture onto the baking sheet and allow to set. When hard, transfer to a plastic bag and break into pieces with a rolling pin. Reserve ½ cup and crush the remainder.

4 Pour half the coffee into a small bowl; sprinkle over the gelatin. Allow to soak for 5 minutes, then place the bowl over a pan of hot water; stir until dissolved.

5 Put the egg yolks, light brown sugar, remaining coffee and liqueur in a bowl over a pan of simmering water. Whisk until thick and foamy, then whisk in the dissolved gelatin.

6 Whip the cream until soft peaks form, then whisk the egg whites until stiff. Fold the crushed praline into the cream, then fold into the coffee mixture. Finally, fold in the egg whites, half at a time.

7 Spoon into the soufflé dish and smooth the top; chill for at least 2 hours, or until set. Put in the freezer for 15–20 minutes before serving. Remove the paper collar by running a warmed metal spatula between the set soufflé and the paper. Whisk the cream for decoration, if using, and place large spoonfuls on top. Decorate with the reserved praline pieces and whole blanched almonds.

TWICE-BAKED MOCHA SOUFFLÉ

THE PERFECT WAY TO END A MEAL, THESE MINI MOCHA SOUFFLÉS CAN BE MADE UP TO 3 HOURS AHEAD, THEN REHEATED JUST BEFORE YOU SERVE THEM.

SERVES SIX

INGREDIENTS

6 tablespoons unsalted
   butter, softened
3½ ounces bittersweet or
   plain chocolate, grated
2 tablespoons ground coffee
1⅔ cup milk
⅓ cup all-purpose flour, sifted
2 tablespoons cocoa, sifted
3 eggs, separated
¼ cup sugar
¾ cup creamy chocolate or coffee
   liqueur, such as Crème de Caçao
   or Kahlúa

1 Preheat the oven to 400°F. Thickly brush six ⅔-cup cylindrical molds or mini pudding bowls with 2 tablespoons of the butter. Coat with 2 ounces of the grated chocolate.

2 Put the ground coffee in a small bowl. Heat the milk until almost boiling and pour over the coffee. Infuse for 4 minutes, then strain, discarding the grounds.

3 Melt the remaining butter in a small pan. Stir in the flour and cocoa to make a roux. Cook for about 1 minute, then gradually add the coffee milk, stirring constantly to make a very thick sauce. Simmer for 2 minutes. Remove from heat and stir in the egg yolks.

VARIATION
Good quality white or milk chocolate can be used instead of plain, if preferred.

4 Cool for 5 minutes, then stir in the remaining chocolate. Whisk the egg whites until stiff, then gradually whisk in the sugar. Stir half into the sauce to lighten, then fold in the remainder.

5 Spoon the mixture into the cylindrical molds and place in a roasting pan. Pour in enough hot water to come two-thirds of the way up the sides of the molds.

6 Bake the soufflés for 15 minutes. Turn them out onto a baking sheet and allow to cool completely.

7 Before serving, spoon 1 tablespoon chocolate or coffee liqueur over each pudding and reheat for 6–7 minutes. Serve on individual plates with the remaining liqueur poured over.

CLASSIC CHOCOLATE AND COFFEE ROULADE

THIS RICH, PLUMP CHOCOLATE ROLL SHOULD BE MADE AT LEAST 12 HOURS BEFORE SERVING, TO ALLOW IT TO SOFTEN. EXPECT THE ROULADE TO CRACK A LITTLE WHEN YOU ROLL IT UP.

SERVES EIGHT

INGREDIENTS
- 7 ounces semisweet chocolate
- 1 cup sugar
- 7 eggs, separated

For the filling
- 1¼ cups heavy cream
- 2 tablespoons cold strong brewed coffee, e.g. mocha-flavored
- 1 tablespoon coffee liqueur, such as Tia Maria or Kahlúa
- ¼ cup confectioners' sugar, for dusting
- little grated chocolate, for sprinkling

1 Preheat the oven to 350°F. Grease and line a 13 x 9-inch jelly roll pan with baking parchment.

2 Break the chocolate into squares and melt in a bowl over a pan of barely simmering water. Remove from heat and allow to cool for 5 minutes.

3 In a large bowl, whisk the sugar and egg yolks until light and fluffy. Stir in the melted chocolate.

4 Whisk the egg whites until stiff but not dry, and then gently fold into the chocolate mixture.

5 Pour the chocolate mixture into the prepared pan, spreading it level with a spatula. Bake for about 25 minutes, until firm. Leave the cake in the pan and cover with a cooling rack, making sure it doesn't touch the cake.

6 Cover the rack with a damp dish towel, then wrap in plastic wrap. Set aside in a cool place for at least 8 hours or overnight, if possible.

7 Dust a large sheet of waxed paper with confectioners' sugar and turn out the roulade onto it. Peel off the lining.

8 To make the filling, whip the heavy cream with the coffee and liqueur until soft peaks form. Spread the cream over the roulade. Starting from one of the short ends, carefully roll it up, using the paper to help.

9 Place the roulade, seam-side down, onto a serving plate; dust with confectioners' sugar and sprinkle with a little grated chocolate before serving.

COOK'S TIP
If desired, decorate the roulade with swirls of whipped cream and chocolate coffee beans or with clusters of raspberries and mint leaves.

MANGO AND COFFEE MERINGUE ROLL

A LIGHT AND FLUFFY ROLL OF MERINGUE IS THE IDEAL CONTRAST TO THE UNSWEETENED FILLING OF COFFEE, MASCARPONE AND JUICY RIPE MANGO.

SERVES SIX TO EIGHT

INGREDIENTS
    4 egg whites
    generous 1 cup superfine sugar
For the filling
    3 tablespoons strong-flavored
      ground coffee
    5 tablespoons milk
    1½ cups mascarpone
    1 ripe mango, cut into ½-inch cubes

COOK'S TIP
If desired, the meringue can be sprinkled with ½ cup of peeled chopped hazelnuts before baking.

1 Preheat the oven to 375°F. Line a 13 x 9-inch jelly roll pan with lightly greased baking parchment. Whisk the egg whites until stiff. Gradually add the sugar, whisking after each addition until thick and glossy.

2 When the meringue is thick and glossy, spoon it into the prepared pan and smooth the surface. Bake for 15 minutes or until firm and golden.

3 Turn the meringue out onto a sheet of baking parchment. Remove the lining paper and set aside until cold.

4 To make the filling, put the coffee in a small bowl. Heat the milk until it is almost boiling and pour over the coffee. Allow to infuse for 4 minutes, then strain through a fine strainer, discarding the coffee grounds.

5 Beat the mascarpone until soft, then gradually beat in the coffee. Spread over the meringue, then sprinkle with the chopped mango.

6 Gently roll up the meringue from one of the short ends, with the help of the baking parchment. Transfer to a serving plate seam-side down. Chill for at least 30 minutes before serving.

GINGERED COFFEE MERINGUES

WHAT COULD BE MORE ENTICING THAN TO BREAK THROUGH THE COATING OF CRISP MERINGUE TO
REVEAL JUST-MELTING COFFEE ICE CREAM ON A MOIST GINGER SPONGE?

SERVES SIX

INGREDIENTS

    10 ounces ready-made ginger cake
    2½ cups coffee ice cream
    4 egg whites
    ¼ teaspoon cream of tartar
    ¾ cup superfine sugar
    2 tablespoons preserved ginger,
      finely chopped

1 Preheat the oven to 450°F. Cut the ginger cake lengthwise into three slices. Cut out two rounds from each slice, using a 2-inch cutter, and put on a baking sheet.

2 Top each cake round with a large scoop of coffee ice cream, then place the baking sheet in the freezer for at least 30 minutes.

3 Whisk the egg whites and cream of tartar until soft peaks form. Gradually add the sugar and continue whisking until the mixture forms stiff peaks. Fold in the preserved ginger.

4 Carefully spoon the meringue and ginger mixture into a pastry bag fitted with a large plain nozzle.

COOK'S TIP
The ice cream is insulated in the oven by the tiny bubbles of air in the meringue, so be sure it is completely covered. Once coated, the ice cream cakes could be frozen until ready to cook.

5 Quickly pipe the meringue over the ice cream, starting from the base and working up to the top.

6 Bake for 3–4 minutes, until the outside of the meringue is crisp and lightly tinged with brown. Serve immediately.

FLOATING ISLANDS

THIS WELL-KNOWN DESSERT GETS ITS NAME FROM THE POACHED MERINGUES SURROUNDED BY A "SEA" OF CRÈME ANGLAISE. THIS VERSION IS GIVEN A TOUCH OF THE EXOTIC WITH THE ADDITION OF STAR ANISE AND IS SERVED WITH A RICH COFFEE SAUCE.

SERVES SIX

INGREDIENTS
For the coffee crème Anglaise
    ⅔ cup milk
    ⅔ cup light cream
    ½ cup strong brewed coffee
    4 egg yolks
    2 tablespoons light brown sugar
    1 teaspoon cornstarch
For the caramel sauce
    ½ cup sugar
For the poached meringues
    2 egg whites
    ¼ cup superfine sugar
    ¼ teaspoon ground star anise
    pinch of salt

1 To make the coffee crème Anglaise, pour the milk, cream and coffee into a pan and heat to boiling point.

2 In a large bowl, combine the egg yolks, brown sugar and cornstarch until creamy. Stir in the hot coffee mixture, then pour the entire mixture back into the pan.

3 Heat for 1–2 minutes, stirring until the sauce thickens. Remove from heat and cool, stirring occasionally.

COOK'S TIP
Once poached, the meringues will keep their shape for up to 2 hours.

4 Cover the bowl containing the sauce with plastic wrap and place in the refrigerator.

5 For the caramel, put the sugar in a small heavy pan with 3 tablespoons water and heat very gently until dissolved. Boil rapidly until the syrup turns a rich golden color. Remove from heat, carefully add 3 tablespoons hot water—it will splutter. Allow to cool.

6 To make the meringues, whisk the egg whites until stiff. Combine the sugar and star anise; add to the egg whites.

7 Pour 1 inch of boiling water into a large frying pan. Add the salt and bring to a gentle simmer. Shape the meringue into small ovals, using two spoons, and add to the water. Poach four or five of the meringues at a time for about 3 minutes, until firm.

8 Remove with a slotted spoon and drain on paper towels. Repeat with the remaining mixture.

9 To serve, spoon a little coffee crème Anglaise onto each serving plate. Float two or three "islands" on top, then drizzle with caramel sauce.

COFFEE MERINGUES WITH ROSE CREAM

THESE SUGARY MERINGUES, WITH CRUSHED ESPRESSO-ROASTED COFFEE BEANS, ARE FILLED WITH A DELICATE ROSE-SCENTED CREAM. LIGHTLY SPRINKLE ROSE PETALS ON TOP FOR A ROMANTIC FINISH.

MAKES TWENTY PAIRS OF MERINGUES

INGREDIENTS
  generous ¼ cup espresso-roasted
    coffee beans
  3 egg whites
  scant 1 cup superfine sugar
  ¼ cup pistachios, coarsely chopped
  few rose petals, for decoration
For the rose cream
  1¼ cups heavy cream
  1 tablespoon confectioners' sugar,
    sifted
  2 teaspoons rose water

1 Preheat the oven to 350°F. Spread the coffee beans on a baking sheet and toast for 8 minutes. Allow to cool, then put in a plastic bag and crush with a rolling pin. Set the oven at 275°F.

2 Whisk the egg whites and sugar in a bowl over a pan of hot water until thick.

3 Remove from heat and continue whisking until the meringue holds stiff peaks. Whisk in the crushed beans.

4 Fill a pastry bag fitted with a large star nozzle with the mixture and pipe about 40 small swirls onto two baking sheets lined with baking parchment. Leave space between the swirls.

5 Sprinkle with the pistachios. Bake the meringues for 2–2½ hours or until dry and crisp, rotating the baking sheets halfway through the cooking time. Allow to cool, then remove from the paper.

6 To make the rose cream, whip the cream, confectioners' sugar and rose water until soft peaks form. Use to sandwich the meringues together in pairs. Arrange on a serving plate decorated with rose petals and serve.

VARIATION
Orange-flower water may be used instead of rose water in the cream and a drop of pink food coloring added, if desired.

COFFEE PAVLOVA WITH TROPICAL FRUITS

BOTH AUSTRALIA AND NEW ZEALAND CLAIM TO HAVE INVENTED THIS FLUFFY MERINGUE NAMED AFTER THE BALLERINA ANNA PAVLOVA. THE SECRET OF SUCCESS IS TO ALLOW THE MERINGUE TO COOL COMPLETELY IN THE OVEN, AS A SUDDEN CHANGE IN TEMPERATURE WILL MAKE IT CRACK.

SERVES SIX TO EIGHT

INGREDIENTS

2 tablespoons ground coffee,
  e.g. mocha orange-flavored
2 tablespoons near-boiling water
3 egg whites
½ teaspoon cream of tartar
scant 1 cup superfine sugar
1 teaspoon cornstarch, sifted

For the filling
⅔ cup heavy cream
1 teaspoon vanilla orange-flower
  water
⅔ cup crème fraîche
1¼ pounds sliced tropical fruits,
  such as mango, papaya and kiwi
1 tablespoon confectioners' sugar

4 Using a long knife or spatula, spoon the meringue mixture onto the baking sheet, spreading to an even 8-inch circle. Make a slight hollow in the middle. Bake for 1 hour, then turn off the heat and allow to cool in the oven.

5 Peel of the lining and transfer the meringue to a plate. To make the filling, whip the cream with the orange-flower water until soft peaks form. Fold in the crème fraîche. Spoon into the meringue. Arrange fruits over the cream and dust with confectioners' sugar.

1 Preheat the oven to 275°F. Draw an 8-inch circle on baking parchment. Place pencil-side down on the baking sheet.

2 Put the coffee in a small bowl and pour the hot water in. Allow to infuse for 4 minutes, then strain through a very fine strainer.

3 Whisk the egg whites with the cream of tartar until stiff, but not dry. Gradually whisk in the sugar until the meringue is stiff and shiny, then quickly whisk in the cornstarch and coffee.

VARIATION
1 pound berries, such as wild or cultivated strawberries, raspberries and blueberries, may be used instead of the tropical fruits, if desired.

FRUIT DESSERTS

If you're looking for color, flavor and freshness and something a little out of the ordinary, opt for one of these fruit and coffee combinations. Fruit always makes for delicious desserts, no matter how simple or grand the meal, but it doesn't have to be chilled. Try steeping oranges in a hot coffee syrup or serve a slice of Maple Pear Cake for pure indulgence.

ORANGES IN HOT COFFEE SYRUP

THIS RECIPE WORKS WELL WITH MOST CITRUS FRUITS; TRY PINK GRAPEFRUIT OR SWEET, PERFUMED CLEMENTINES, PEELED BUT LEFT WHOLE, FOR A CHANGE.

SERVES SIX

INGREDIENTS
  6 medium oranges
  1 cup sugar
  ¼ cup cold water
  scant ½ cup boiling water
  scant ½ cup fresh strong
    brewed coffee
  ½ cup pistachios, chopped (optional)

COOK'S TIP
Choose a pan in which the oranges will fit in a single layer.

1 Finely pare the zest from one orange, shred and reserve the zest. Peel the remaining oranges. Cut each one crosswise into slices, then re-form with a toothpick through the center.

2 Put the sugar and cold water in a heavy pan. Heat gently until the sugar dissolves, then bring to a boil and cook until the syrup turns pale gold.

3 Remove from heat and carefully pour the boiling water into the pan. Return to the heat until the syrup has dissolved in the water. Stir in the coffee.

4 Add the oranges and the shredded zest to the coffee syrup. Simmer for 15–20 minutes, turning the oranges once during cooking. Sprinkle with pistachios, if using, and serve hot.

FRESH FIG COMPOTE

LIGHTLY POACHING FIGS IN A VANILLA AND COFFEE SYRUP BRINGS OUT THEIR WONDERFUL FLAVOR.

SERVES FOUR TO SIX

INGREDIENTS
  1⅔ cups brewed coffee
  ½ cup honey
  1 vanilla bean
  12 slightly underripe fresh figs
  plain yogurt, to serve (optional)

COOK'S TIPS
• Rinse and dry the vanilla bean; it can be used several times.
• Figs come in three main varieties—red, white and black—and all three are suitable for cooking. Naturally high in sugar, they are sweet and succulent and complement well the stronger flavors of coffee and vanilla.

1 Choose a frying pan with a lid, large enough to hold the figs in a single layer. Pour in the coffee and add the honey.

2 Split the vanilla bean lengthwise and scrape the seeds into the pan. Add the vanilla bean, then bring to a boil. Bring the syrup to a rapid boil and cook until reduced to about ¾ cup. Set aside to cool.

3 Wash the figs and pierce the skins several times with a sharp skewer. Cut in half and add to the syrup. Lower the heat, cover and simmer for 5 minutes. Remove the figs from the syrup with a slotted spoon and set aside to cool.

4 Strain the syrup over the figs. Allow to stand at room temperature for 1 hour before serving with yogurt, desired.

MAPLE PEAR CAKE

CLOVES ADD A DISTINCTIVE FRAGRANT FLAVOR TO THIS HAZELNUT, PEAR AND COFFEE CAKE.

SERVES SIX

INGREDIENTS
    2 tablespoons ground coffee,
      e.g. hazelnut-flavored
    1 tablespoon almost-boiling water
    ½ cup toasted peeled hazelnuts
    4 ripe pears
    juice of ½ orange
    8 tablespoons butter, softened
    generous ½ cup sugar, plus an extra
      1 tablespoon, for baking
    2 eggs, beaten
    ½ cup self-rising flour, sifted
    pinch of ground cloves
    8 whole cloves, optional
    3 tablespoons maple syrup
    fine strips of orange zest,
      to decorate
For the orange cream
    1¼ cups whipping cream
    1 tablespoon confectioners' sugar,
      sifted
    finely grated zest of ½ orange

1 Preheat the oven to 350°F. Lightly grease an 8-inch cake pan. Put the ground coffee in a small bowl and pour the water over. Allow to infuse for 4 minutes, then strain through a fine strainer.

COOK'S TIP
If you can't find ready-toasted peeled hazelnuts, prepare your own. Toast under a hot broiler for 3–4 minutes, turning frequently until well browned. Rub off the skins and cool before grinding.

2 Grind the hazelnuts in a coffee grinder until fine. Peel, halve and core the pears. Thinly slice across the pear halves part of the way through. Brush with orange juice.

3 Beat the butter and the generous ½ cup sugar together in a large bowl until very light and fluffy. Gradually beat in the eggs, then fold in the flour, ground cloves, hazelnuts and coffee. Spoon the batter into the pan and level the surface.

4 Pat the pears dry on paper towels, then arrange in the cake batter, cut side down.

5 Lightly press 2 whole cloves, if using, into each pear half. Brush the pears with 1 tablespoon of the maple syrup.

6 Sprinkle the pears with 1 tablespoon of the sugar. Bake for 45–50 minutes or until firm and well-risen.

7 While the cake is baking, make the orange cream. Whip the cream, confectioners' sugar and orange zest until soft peaks form. Spoon into a serving dish and chill until needed.

8 Allow the cake to cool for about 10 minutes in the pan, then remove and place on a serving plate. Lightly brush with the remaining maple syrup before decorating with orange zest. Serve warm with the orange cream.

COFFEE CRÊPES with PEACHES and CREAM

JUICY GOLDEN PEACHES AND CREAM CONJURE UP THE SWEET TASTE OF SUMMER. HERE THEY ARE DELICIOUS AS THE FILLING FOR THESE LIGHT COFFEE CRÊPES.

SERVES SIX

INGREDIENTS
⅔ cup all-purpose flour
¼ cup buckwheat flour
¼ teaspoon salt
1 egg, beaten
scant 1 cup milk
1 tablespoon butter, melted
scant ½ cup strong brewed coffee
sunflower oil, for frying
For the filling
6 ripe peaches
1¼ cups heavy cream
1 tablespoon Amaretto liqueur
1 cup mascarpone
generous ¼ cup superfine sugar
2 tablespoons confectioners' sugar,
  for dusting

1 Sift the flours and salt into a mixing bowl. Make a well in the middle and add the egg, half the milk and the melted butter. Gradually mix in the flour, beating until smooth, then beat in the remaining milk and coffee.

2 Heat a drizzle of oil in a 6–8-inch crêpe pan. Pour in just enough batter to thinly cover the bottom of the pan. Cook for 2–3 minutes, until the underside is golden brown, then flip over and cook the other side.

COOK'S TIP
To keep the pancakes warm while you make the rest, cover them with tinfoil and place the plate over a pan of barely simmering water.

3 Slide the crêpe out of the pan onto a plate. Continue making crêpes until all the mixture is used, stacking and interleaving with waxed paper.

4 To make the filling, halve the peaches and remove the pits. Cut into thick slices. Whip the cream and Amaretto liqueur until soft peaks form. Beat the mascarpone with the sugar until smooth. Beat 2 tablespoons of the cream into the mascarpone, then fold in the remainder.

5 Spoon a little of the Amaretto cream onto one half of each pancake and top with peach slices. Gently fold the pancake over and dust with confectioners' sugar. Serve immediately.

PLUM AND RUM BABAS

A POLISH KING THOUGHT UP THESE SPONGY YEAST CAKES AFTER HEARING THE STORY OF ALI BABA.
SOAKED IN A COFFEE AND RUM SYRUP, THEIR CENTERS ARE FILLED WITH JUICY PLUMS.

SERVES SIX

INGREDIENTS
   5 tablespoons unsalted
     butter, softened
   1 cup strong all-purpose flour
   pinch of salt
   1½ teaspoons active dry yeast
   2 tablespoons light brown sugar
   2 eggs, beaten
   3 tablespoons warm milk
   crème fraîche, to serve
For the syrup
   generous ½ cup sugar
   ½ cup water
   1 pound plums, halved, pitted and
     thickly sliced
   ½ cup brewed coffee
   3 tablespoons dark rum

4 Cover with plastic wrap and let rise for 40 minutes. Cut the remaining butter into cubes and mix into the dough. Put the pans on a baking sheet and drop the dough into the molds. Cover with oiled plastic wrap and set aside until the dough has almost risen to the top. Remove the plastic wrap and bake for 15–20 minutes.

5 Meanwhile, make the syrup. Put 2 tablespoons of the sugar in a pan with the water. Add the plums and cook over low heat until barely tender; remove with a slotted spoon. Add the remaining sugar and coffee to the pan. Heat gently until dissolved, but do not boil. Remove from heat and stir in the rum.

6 Turn out the babas onto a wire rack and allow to cool for 5 minutes. Dunk them in the warm syrup until well soaked. Return them to the wire rack with a plate underneath to catch any drips. Allow to cool completely.

7 Put the babas on a serving plate and fill the centers with the sliced plums. Spoon a little extra syrup over each and serve with crème fraîche.

1 Preheat the oven to 375°F. Thickly brush six 3½-in bundt pans with 1 tablespoon of the butter.

2 Sift the flour and salt into a mixing bowl and stir in the yeast and light brown sugar.

3 Make a well in the middle and add the eggs and warm milk. Beat for about 5 minutes with a wooden spoon to make a very sticky dough that is fairly smooth and elastic.

COOK'S TIP
The babas may also be split in half horizontally, filled with whipped cream and sandwiched back together.

COCONUT AND COFFEE TRIFLE

DARK COFFEE SPONGE, LACED WITH LIQUEUR, COCONUT CUSTARD AND A COFFEE CREAM TOPPING MAKES THIS A LAVISH DESSERT. SERVE IN A LARGE GLASS BOWL FOR MAXIMUM IMPACT.

SERVES SIX TO EIGHT

INGREDIENTS
For the coffee sponge
 3 tablespoons strong-flavored
  ground coffee
 3 tablespoons almost-boiling water
 2 eggs
 ¼ cup dark brown sugar
 ⅓ cup self-rising flour, sifted
 1½ tablespoons hazelnut or
  sunflower oil
For the coconut custard
 1⅔ cup canned coconut milk
 3 eggs
 3 tablespoons sugar
 2 teaspoons cornstarch
For the filling and topping
 2 medium bananas
 ¼ cup coffee liqueur, such as
  Tia Maria or Kahlúa
 1¼ cups heavy cream
 2 tablespoons confectioners' sugar,
  sifted
 ribbons of fresh coconut, to decorate

1 Preheat the oven to 325°F. Grease and line a 7-inch square pan with waxed paper.

2 Put the coffee in a cup. Pour the hot water over and allow to infuse for 4 minutes. Strain through a fine strainer, discarding the grounds.

3 Whisk the eggs and dark brown sugar in a large bowl until the whisk leaves a trail when lifted.

4 Gently fold in the flour, followed by 1 tablespoon of the coffee and the oil. Spoon the mixture into the pan and bake for 20 minutes, until firm. Turn out onto a wire rack, remove the lining paper and allow to cool.

5 To make the coconut custard, heat the coconut milk in a saucepan until it is almost boiling.

6 Whisk the eggs, sugar and cornstarch together until frothy. Pour in the hot coconut milk, whisking all the time. Add to the pan and heat gently, stirring for 1–2 minutes, until the custard thickens, but do not boil. Cool for 10 minutes, stirring occasionally.

7 Cut the coffee sponge into 2-inch squares and arrange in the bottom of a large glass bowl. Slice the bananas and arrange on top of the sponge. Drizzle the coffee liqueur on top. Pour the custard over and set aside until cold.

8 Whip the cream with the remaining coffee and confectioners' sugar until soft peaks form. Spoon the cream over the custard. Cover and chill for several hours. Sprinkle with ribbons of fresh coconut before serving.

COOK'S TIP
To make coconut ribbons, use a vegetable peeler to cut thin ribbons from the meat of a fresh coconut, or buy shredded coconut and toast until it is pale golden.

FLAMBÉED BANANAS WITH CARIBBEAN COFFEE SAUCE

THIS DESSERT HAS ALL THE FLAVOR OF THE CARIBBEAN: BANANAS, DARK SUGAR, COFFEE AND RUM.

SERVES FOUR TO SIX

INGREDIENTS
    6 bananas
    3 tablespoons butter
    ¼ cup dark brown sugar
    ¼ cup strong brewed coffee
    ¼ cup dark rum
    vanilla ice cream, to serve

1 Peel the bananas and cut in half lengthwise. Melt the butter in a large frying pan over medium heat. Add the bananas and cook for 3 minutes, carefully turning halfway through cooking time.

COOK'S TIP
These hot bananas taste equally good served with coconut or coffee ice cream.

2 Sprinkle the sugar over the bananas, then add the coffee. Continue cooking, stirring occasionally, for 2–3 minutes or until the bananas are tender.

3 Pour the rum into the pan and bring to a boil. With a long match or taper and tilting the pan, ignite the rum. As soon as the flames subside, serve the bananas with vanilla ice cream.

GRILLED NECTARINES WITH COFFEE MASCARPONE FILLING

THIS SIMPLE DESSERT IS PERFECT FOR NECTARINES THAT ARE STILL SLIGHTLY HARD, AS THEY'RE BROILED WITH A DELICIOUS HONEY AND BUTTER GLAZE AND FILLED WITH CHILLED COFFEE CREAM.

SERVES FOUR

INGREDIENTS
    ½ cup mascarpone
    3 tablespoons cold very strong
      brewed coffee
    4 nectarines
    1 tablespoon butter, melted
      and cooled
    3 tablespoons honey
    pinch of ground allspice
    ¼ cup slivered brazil nuts

1 Beat the mascarpone until softened, then gradually mix in the cold brewed coffee. Cover with plastic wrap and chill for 20 minutes.

2 Cut the nectarines in half and remove the pits. In a small bowl, mix the butter, 2 tablespoons of the honey and allspice. Brush the spicy butter all over the cut surfaces.

3 Arrange the nectarines, cut-side up on a tinfoil-lined broiler pan. Cook under a hot broiler for 2–3 minutes. Add the brazil nuts to the broiler pan for the last minute of cooking and toast until golden.

4 Put a spoonful of the chilled cheese mixture in the center of each hot nectarine. Drizzle with the remaining honey and sprinkle with the toasted brazil nuts before serving.

COOK'S TIP
If possible, choose a fragrant honey for this dessert: orange blossom and rosemary are both delicious.

CARAMELIZED APPLES

A TRADITIONAL DESSERT WITH A DIFFERENCE—BAKED APPLES BATHED IN A RICH COFFEE SYRUP.

SERVES SIX

INGREDIENTS
  6 apples, peeled, but left whole
  4 tablespoons unsalted butter,
    melted and cooled
  ½ cup sugar
  ¼ teaspoon ground cinnamon
  6 tablespoons strong brewed coffee
  whipped cream, to serve

COOK'S TIP
This recipe is equally good made with
pears, but reduce the cooking time by
10–15 minutes and use allspice instead
of the cinnamon.

1 Preheat the oven to 350°F. Cut a thin
slice from the bottom of each apple to
give them a flat base. Using a pastry
brush, thickly coat each apple with
melted butter.

2 Mix the sugar and cinnamon in a
shallow dish. Holding each apple by
its stalk, roll in the mixture to coat.

3 Arrange the apples in a shallow
baking dish into which they just fit.
Stand them upright.

4 Pour the coffee into the dish, then
sprinkle over any remaining sugar
mixture. Bake the apples for 40 minutes,
basting with the coffee two or three
times throughout. Baste a last time,
then pour the juices into a small pan,
returning the apples to the oven.

5 Boil the juices rapidly until syrupy
and reduced to about ¼ cup. Pour over
the apples and cook for 10 more
minutes or until the apples are tender.
Serve hot with a spoonful of cream.

SUMMER BERRIES WITH COFFEE SABAYON

*FOR A LIGHT AND DELICIOUSLY REFRESHING FINALE, SERVE A PLATTER OF FRESH SUMMER FRUIT WITH
A FLUFFY COFFEE SAUCE, WHICH HAS THE ADDED ADVANTAGE OF BEING DELIGHTFULLY EASY TO MAKE.*

SERVES SIX

INGREDIENTS
  6–8 cups mixed berries such as
    raspberries, blueberries and
    strawberries (hulled and halved,
    if large)
  5 egg yolks
  scant ½ cup sugar
  ¼ cup brewed coffee
  2 tablespoons coffee liqueur,
    such as Tia Maria or Kahlúa
  mint leaves, to decorate (optional)
  2 tablespoons confectioners' sugar,
    to dust

COOK'S TIP
Don't let the water get too hot when
making the sauce, or it may curdle.

1 Arrange the fruit on a serving platter
and decorate with mint leaves, if
desired. Dust with confectioners' sugar.

2 Whisk the egg yolks and sugar in a
bowl over a pan of simmering water
until the mixture begins to thicken.

3 Gradually add the coffee and liqueur,
pouring in a thin, continuous stream
and whisking constantly. Continue
whisking until the sauce is thick and
fluffy. Serve warm or allow to cool,
whisking occasionally, and serve
cold with the fruit.

FROZEN DESSERTS

Frozen desserts are an ideal choice for all occasions, as they can be made in advance, then stored in the freezer. In this chapter, you'll find smooth, velvety ice creams and refreshing sorbets. Some are only part of the dessert, such as in Dark Chocolate and Coffee Mousse Cake, a rich chocolate cake with an ice cream center.

CINNAMON AND COFFEE SWIRL ICE CREAM

LIGHT ICE CREAM SUBTLY SPICED WITH CINNAMON AND RIPPLED WITH A SWEET COFFEE SYRUP.

SERVES SIX

INGREDIENTS
  1¼ cups light cream
  1 cinnamon stick
  4 egg yolks
  ¾ cup sugar
  1¼ cups heavy cream
For the coffee syrup
  3 tablespoons ground coffee
  3 tablespoons almost-boiling water
  ½ cup sugar
  ¼ cup water

1 Pour the light cream into a small pan and add the cinnamon stick. Slowly bring to a boil. Turn off the heat, cover with a lid and allow to infuse for 30 minutes. Bring back to a boil and remove the cinnamon stick.

2 Whisk the yolks and sugar until light. Pour the hot cream over the egg mixture, whisking. Return to the pan and stir over low heat for 1–2 minutes, until it thickens. Allow to cool.

3 Whip the heavy cream until peaks form and fold into the custard. Pour into a container and freeze for 3 hours.

4 Meanwhile, to make the syrup, put the coffee in a bowl and pour the hot water over. Allow to infuse for 4 minutes, then strain though a strainer.

COOK'S TIP
Make sure that the cinnamon ice cream is sufficiently frozen before adding the coffee syrup.

5 Gently heat the sugar and cold water in a pan until completely dissolved. Bring to a boil and gently simmer for 5 minutes. Cool, then stir in the coffee.

6 Turn the cinnamon ice cream into a chilled bowl and briefly stir to break down the ice crystals.

7 Spoon a third back into the container and drizzle some of the coffee syrup over. Repeat in this way until all is used.

8 Drag a skewer through the mixture a few times to achieve a marbled effect. Freeze for 4 hours or until solid. Allow to soften slightly before serving.

TOASTED NUT AND COFFEE ICE CREAM IN BRANDY SNAP BASKETS

SCOOPS OF CRUSHED CARAMEL AND TOASTED NUT ICE CREAM ARE SERVED IN CRUNCHY BASKETS, THEN DRIZZLED WITH A WARM COFFEE AND COGNAC SAUCE.

SERVES SIX

INGREDIENTS
    ½ cup whole nuts, such as blanched
        almonds and hazelnuts
    ½ cup sugar
    1 vanilla bean, split
    2 tablespoons ground coffee
    scant 1 cup heavy cream
    1¼ cups plain yogurt
    6 brandy snap baskets, to serve
For the coffee and cognac sauce
    ½ cup light brown sugar
    ¼ cup hot water
    ½ cup strong brewed coffee
    ¼ cup cognac

2 Pour onto an oiled baking sheet to cool and harden. Crush to a fine powder. Put the vanilla, coffee and cream in a pan. Heat to almost-boiling, turn off the heat, cover and infuse.

3 After 15 minutes, strain through a strainer and allow to cool. Stir the coffee cream into the yogurt with the crushed nut mixture. Transfer to a freezerproof container and freeze for 4 hours.

4 To make the sauce, heat the sugar and water in a small heavy pan over low heat until melted. Simmer for 3 minutes. Cool slightly, then stir in the coffee and cognac.

5 Meanwhile, allow the ice cream to soften in the refrigerator for 15 minutes. Scoop into the brandy snap baskets and serve immediately with the warm coffee and cognac sauce.

1 Put the whole nuts and sugar in a large heavy pan and heat gently until the sugar caramelizes to a light golden brown, shaking the pan only occasionally.

COOK'S TIP
To make brandy snap baskets: in a bowl, gently melt 4 tablespoons butter, ¼ cup light brown sugar and ¼ cup light corn syrup. Stir in ½ cup sifted all-purpose flour and 1 teaspoon brandy. Drop well-spaced teaspoons onto oiled baking sheets. Bake in a preheated oven at 325°F for about 8 minutes. Cool for 1 minute, then lift with a metal spatula and mold over the base of an inverted glass.

COFFEE ICE CREAM

FRESHLY GROUND COFFEE GIVES THIS CLASSIC ICE CREAM A DISTINCTIVE AND SOPHISTICATED FLAVOR.
CHOOSE A DARK-ROASTED BEAN TO ENSURE A RICH, GLOSSY COLOR TO THE ICE CREAM.

SERVES EIGHT TO TEN

INGREDIENTS
    4 tablespoons cup dark-roasted
      ground coffee
    2½ cups milk
    scant 1 cup light brown sugar
    6 egg yolks
    2 cups whipping cream

1 Put the coffee in a pitcher. Heat the milk in a saucepan to almost-boiling and pour over the coffee. Allow to stand for 4 minutes.

2 Meanwhile, in a large bowl, beat the sugar and egg yolks until light. Pour the milk over, beating constantly. Strain the mixture back into the pan through a fine strainer.

3 Cook the custard over low heat for 1–2 minutes, stirring until it coats the back of a wooden spoon. Do not boil. Pour into a shallow freezer container and allow to cool, stirring occasionally.

COOK'S TIP
If using an ice cream maker, do not whip the cream; instead, stir it into the coffee custard before adding to the machine.

4 Freeze for about 2 hours, then turn into a bowl and stir with a fork until smooth. Whip the cream until peaks form and fold into the frozen mixture.

5 Return to the freezer for 1 more hour, then turn out and stir again. Finally, freeze for 3–4 hours, until solid. Transfer to the refrigerator for 20 minutes, before scooping and serving.

CAPPUCCINO CONES

PRETTY WHITE AND DARK CHOCOLATE CONES ARE FILLED WITH SWIRLS OF CAPPUCCINO CREAM AND
TOPPED WITH A LIGHT DUSTING OF COCOA POWDER.

SERVES SIX

INGREDIENTS
    4 ounces each good quality
      semisweet and white chocolate
For the cappuccino cream
    2 tablespoons ground espresso or
      other strong-flavored coffee
    2 tablespoons almost-boiling water
    1¼ cups heavy cream
    3 tablespoons confectioners' sugar,
      sifted
    unsweetened cocoa powder for dusting

1 Cut nine 5 x 4-inch rectangles from baking parchment, then cut each rectangle in half diagonally to make 18 triangles. Roll up each to make a cone and secure with tape.

2 Heat the semisweet chocolate in a bowl over a pan of hot water until melted. Using a small pastry brush, thickly brush the insides of half the paper cones with chocolate. Chill until set. Repeat with the white chocolate. Carefully peel away the paper and keep the cones in the refrigerator until needed.

3 To make the cappuccino cream, put the coffee in a small bowl. Pour the hot water over. Allow to infuse for 4 minutes, then strain though a fine strainer into a bowl. Allow to cool. Add the cream and sugar and whisk until soft peaks form. Spoon into a pastry bag fitted with a medium star nozzle.

4 Pipe the cream into the chocolate cones. Put on a baking sheet and freeze for at least 2 hours, or until solid. Arrange on individual plates, allowing three cones per person and dusting with the cocoa powder before serving.

COOK'S TIP
Make sure, when melting the chocolate, that the water doesn't boil, or the chocolate will overheat and stiffen.

MAPLE COFFEE AND PISTACHIO BOMBES

REAL MAPLE SYRUP TASTES INFINITELY BETTER THAN THE SYNTHETIC VARIETIES AND IS WELL WORTH SEARCHING FOR. HERE IT SWEETENS THE DARK COFFEE CENTER OF THESE PRETTY PISTACHIO BOMBES.

SERVES SIX

INGREDIENTS
For the pistachio ice cream
   ¼ cup sugar
   ¼ cup water
   6-ounce can evaporated
    milk, chilled
   ½ cup shelled and peeled pistachios,
    finely chopped
   drop of green food coloring (optional)
   scant 1 cup whipping cream
For the maple coffee centers
   2 tablespoons ground coffee
   ⅔ cup light cream
   ¼ cup maple syrup
   2 egg yolks
   1 teaspoon cornstarch
   ⅔ cup whipping cream

1 Put six ¾-cup mini pudding bowls or cylindrical molds into the freezer to chill. Put the sugar and water in a heavy saucepan and heat gently until dissolved. Bring to a boil and simmer for 3 minutes.

2 Cool, then stir in the chilled evaporated milk, pistachios and coloring, if using. Lightly whip the cream until it forms soft peaks and blend into the mixture.

3 Pour the mixture into a freezerproof container and freeze for at least 2 hours. Whisk the ice cream until smooth, then freeze for another 2 hours or until frozen, but not solid.

4 To make the centers, put the ground coffee in a pitcher. Heat the light cream to almost-boiling and pour over the coffee. Allow to infuse for 4 minutes. Whisk the maple syrup, egg yolks and cornstarch together. Strain the hot coffee cream over the egg mixture, whisking constantly. Return to the pan and cook gently for 1–2 minutes, until the custard thickens. Allow to cool, stirring occasionally.

5 Meanwhile, line the molds with the ice cream, keeping the thickness as even as possible right up to the rim. Freeze until the ice cream is firm again.

6 Beat the cream until peaks form. Fold into the custard. Spoon into the middle of the molds. Cover and freeze for 2 hours. Unmold and serve immediately.

FROSTED RASPBERRY AND COFFEE TERRINE

A WHITE CHOCOLATE AND RASPBERRY LAYER AND A CONTRASTING SMOOTH COFFEE LAYER MAKE THIS ATTRACTIVE LOOKING DESSERT DOUBLY DELICIOUS.

SERVES SIX TO EIGHT

INGREDIENTS
2 tablespoons ground coffee,
  e.g. mocha orange-flavored
1 cup milk
4 eggs, separated
¼ cup sugar
2 tablespoons cornstarch
⅔ cup heavy cream
5 ounces white chocolate,
  coarsely chopped
⅔ cup raspberries
shavings of white chocolate and
  unsweetened cocoa powder,
  to decorate

1 Line a 6¼-cup loaf pan with plastic wrap and put in the freezer to chill. Put the ground coffee in a cup. Heat scant ½ cup of the milk to almost-boiling and pour over the coffee. Allow to infuse.

2 Blend the egg yolks, sugar and cornstarch together in a saucepan and stir in the remaining milk and the cream. Bring to the boil, stirring constantly, until thickened.

3 Divide the hot mixture between two bowls and add the white chocolate to one, stirring until melted. Strain the coffee through a fine strainer into the other bowl and mix well. Set aside until cool, stirring occasionally.

COOK'S TIP
After decorating, allow the terrine to soften in the refrigerator for 20 minutes before slicing and serving.

4 Whisk two of the egg whites until stiff. Fold into the coffee custard. Spoon into the pan and freeze for 30 minutes. Whisk remaining whites and fold into the chocolate mixture with the raspberries.

5 Spoon into the pan and level before freezing for 4 hours. Turn the terrine out onto a flat serving plate and peel off the plastic wrap. Cover with chocolate shavings and dust with the cocoa powder.

COFFEE AND MINTY-LEMON SORBET

THE FLAVORS OF FRESH MINT, TANGY LEMON AND AROMATIC COFFEE ARE COMBINED IN THIS DELICIOUS ICY SORBET. THE LEMON SHELLS ARE AN EASY, BUT PRETTY, SUMMERY DECORATIVE TOUCH.

SERVES SIX

INGREDIENTS
    generous ½ cup sugar
    1⅔ cups water
    ½ ounce fresh mint leaves
    2 tablespoons coffee liqueur, such as
       Tia Maria or Kahlúa
    6 lemons
    1 egg white
    sprigs of fresh mint, to decorate

1 Put the sugar in a large heavy saucepan with the water and heat gently until dissolved, stirring occasionally. Bring to a boil, and simmer for 5 minutes.

COOK'S TIP
Fresh fruit sorbets will keep in the freezer for up to 2 months, but are best eaten within several days of making.

2 Remove from heat, add the mint leaves, stir and allow to cool. Strain into a pitcher and stir in the liqueur.

3 Cut a thin slice from the base of each lemon so that they will stand upright, being careful not to cut through the pith. Cut the tops off the lemons and keep for lids. Scrape out the lemon flesh and squeeze the juice. Strain the juice into the mint and coffee syrup.

4 Pour into a freezerproof container and freeze for 3 hours. Stir to break down the ice crystals, then freeze for 1 more hour. Whisk the egg white until stiff, then stir into the ice. Spoon into the lemon shells and replace the lids.

5 Place upright on a tray and freeze for 2 hours, until solid. Transfer to the refrigerator 5 minutes before serving, to soften. Decorate with sprigs of mint.

ESPRESSO GRANITA

THIS FAMOUS FROZEN ITALIAN ICE MAKES A REFRESHING FINISH TO A RICH MEAL.

SERVES SIX

INGREDIENTS
    ½ cup sugar
    2½ cups espresso or other strong-
       flavored coffee
    whipped cream, to serve (optional)

COOK'S TIPS
• Don't stir the granita too vigorously—it should have a rough granular texture, rather than a smooth one like a sorbet.
• After step 3, the granita can either be served at that stage or covered and stored in the freezer for up to 2 weeks.

1 Add the sugar to the hot coffee and stir until dissolved. Allow to cool, then pour into a 3¾-cup shallow freezer container.

2 Freeze for at least 3 hours or until ice crystals form around the edges. Stir with a fork, then return to the freezer for another hour.

3 Stir the mixture again with a fork and re-freeze. Repeat until the mixture is frozen and there is no liquid.

4 Transfer the granita to the refrigerator 20 minutes before serving. Break up the ice crystals with a fork and serve in glasses, topped with whipped cream, if desired.

ICED COFFEE MOUSSE <u>IN A</u> CHOCOLATE BOWL

A DARK CHOCOLATE BOWL IS FILLED WITH A LIGHT, ICED COFFEE MOUSSE. THE RESULT IS A DRAMATIC DESSERT, BUT IS NOT DIFFICULT TO MAKE.

<u>SERVES EIGHT</u>

INGREDIENTS
  1 envelope powdered gelatin
  ¼ cup very strong brewed coffee
  2 tablespoons coffee liqueur, such as
    Tia Maria or Kahlúa
  3 eggs, separated
  scant ½ cup sugar
  ⅔ cup whipping cream,
    lightly whipped
For the chocolate bowl
  8 ounces semisweet chocolate
    squares, plus extra for decoration

1 Grease and line a deep
7-inch springform cake pan with
baking parchment.

2 Melt the chocolate in a bowl over a
pan of simmering water. Using a pastry
brush, brush a layer of chocolate over the
bottom of the pan and about 3 inches up
the sides, finishing with a ragged edge.
Allow the chocolate to set before
repeating. Put in the freezer to harden.

3 Sprinkle the gelatin over the coffee in
a bowl and allow to soften for
5 minutes. Put the bowl over a pan of
simmering water; stir until dissolved.
Remove from heat and stir in the
liqueur. Beat the egg yolks and sugar in
a bowl over the simmering water until
thick enough to leave a trail. Remove
from the pan and beat until cool. Whisk
the egg whites until stiff.

4 Pour the dissolved gelatin into the
egg yolk mixture in a thin stream,
stirring gently. Chill in the refrigerator
for 20 minutes or until just beginning to
set, then fold in the cream, followed by
the whisked egg whites.

5 Remove the chocolate bowl from the
freezer and peel off the lining. Put it
back in the pan, then pour in the
mousse. Return to the freezer for at least
3 hours. To serve, remove from the pan
and place on a plate. Allow to soften in
the refrigerator for 40 minutes before
serving. Decorate with grated chocolate.
Use a knife dipped in hot water and
wipe dry to cut into slices to serve.

DARK CHOCOLATE <u>AND</u> COFFEE MOUSSE CAKE

THIS DOUBLE TREAT WILL PROVE IRRESISTIBLE—SPONGE CAKE FILLED WITH CREAMY COFFEE MOUSSE.

<u>SERVES EIGHT</u>

INGREDIENTS
    4 eggs
    generous ½ cup sugar
    ⅔ cup all-purpose flour, sifted
    ¼ cup unsweetened cocoa
      powder, sifted
    ¼ cup coffee liqueur, such as
      Tia Maria or Kahlúa
    confectioners' sugar, to dust
For the coffee mousse
    2 tablespoons dark-roasted
      ground coffee beans
    1½ cups heavy cream
    generous ½ cup sugar
    ½ cup water
    4 egg yolks

1 Preheat the oven to 350°F. Grease and line the bottoms of an 8-inch square and a 9-inch round cake pan with baking parchment. Put the eggs and sugar in a bowl over a pan of hot water and whisk until thick.

2 Remove from heat and whisk until thick enough to leave a trail when the whisk is lifted. Gently fold in the flour and cocoa. Pour a third of the mixture into the square pan and the remainder into the round pan. Bake the square cake for 15 minutes and the round for 30 minutes, until firm.

3 Cool on a wire rack before slicing the round cake in half horizontally. Place the bottom half back in the pan. Sprinkle with half the liqueur.

4 Trim the edges of the square cake, cut into 4 equal strips and use to line the sides of the pan.

5 To make the mousse, put the coffee in a bowl. Heat ¼ cup of the cream to almost-boiling and pour over the coffee. Allow to infuse for 4 minutes, then strain through a fine strainer.

6 Gently heat the sugar and water until dissolved. Increase the heat and boil steadily until the syrup reaches 225°F. Cool for 5 minutes, then pour onto the egg yolks, whisking until the mixture is very thick.

7 Add the coffee cream to the remaining cream and whip until soft peaks form. Fold into the egg mixture. Spoon into the cake shell and freeze for 20 minutes. Sprinkle the remaining liqueur over the second cake half and place on top of the mousse. Cover and freeze for 4 hours. Remove from the pan and dust with confectioners' sugar.

COOK'S TIP
Cover the seams of the cake with swirls of piped whipped cream and decorate with chocolate coffee beans, if desired.

CAKES
AND
TORTES

From simple sponges to elaborate tortes and velvety cheesecakes, these are cakes to rival any store-bought confection. Some, such as Coffee Almond Marsala Cake, are perfect with mid-morning coffee. Others, like Coffee Chocolate Mousse Cake and Cappuccino Torte, make unforgettable dinner party desserts.

COCONUT COFFEE CAKE

COCONUT AND COFFEE ARE NATURAL PARTNERS, AS THESE LITTLE SQUARES OF FROSTED CAKE PROVE.

SERVES NINE

INGREDIENTS
  3 tablespoons ground coffee
  5 tablespoons almost-boiling milk
  2 tablespoons sugar
  ⅔ cup light corn syrup
  6 tablespoons butter
  ½ cup dried coconut
  1½ cups all-purpose flour
  ½ teaspoon baking soda
  2 eggs, lightly beaten
For the frosting
  8 tablespoons butter, softened
  2 cups confectioners' sugar, sifted
  ⅓ cup shredded or flaked
    coconut, toasted

1 Preheat the oven to 325°F. Grease and line the bottom of an 8-inch square pan.

2 Put the ground coffee in a small bowl and pour the hot milk over. Allow to infuse for 4 minutes, then strain through a fine strainer.

3 Heat the sugar, light corn syrup, butter and dried coconut in a pan, stirring with a wooden spoon, until completely melted.

4 Sift the flour and baking soda together and stir into the mixture, along with the eggs and 3 tablespoons of the coffee-flavored milk.

5 Spoon the mixture into the prepared pan and level the top. Bake for 40–50 minutes, until well-risen and firm. Allow the cake to cool in the pan for about 10 minutes, before running a knife around the edges to loosen. Turn out and cool on a wire rack.

6 To make the frosting, beat the softened butter until smooth then gradually beat in the confectioners' sugar and remaining coffee milk to give a soft consistency. Spread over the top of the cake and decorate with toasted coconut. Cut into 2-inch squares to serve.

VARIATION
Substitute ½ cup chopped pecans for the dried coconut and decorate the squares with pecan halves dusted with confectioners' sugar.

MOCHA SPONGE CAKE

THE YEMENI CITY OF MOCHA WAS ONCE CONSIDERED TO BE THE COFFEE CAPITAL OF THE WORLD, AND STILL PRODUCES A COFFEE THAT TASTES A LITTLE LIKE CHOCOLATE. TODAY "MOCHA" MAY REFER TO THE VARIETY OF COFFEE OR MEAN A COMBINATION OF COFFEE OR CHOCOLATE, AS IN THIS RECIPE.

SERVES TEN

INGREDIENTS

1½ tablespoons strong-flavored
    ground coffee
¾ cup milk
8 tablespoons butter
½ cup light brown sugar
1 egg, lightly beaten
1⅔ cups self-rising flour
1 teaspoon baking soda
¼ cup creamy liqueur, such as
    Baileys or Irish Velvet
For the glossy chocolate confectioners'
7 ounces semisweet chocolate,
    broken into pieces
6 tablespoons unsalted butter, cubed
½ cup heavy cream

1 Preheat the oven to 350°F. Grease and line a 7-inch round cake pan with waxed paper.

2 To make the cake, put the coffee in a cup. Heat the milk to almost-boiling and pour over. Allow to infuse for 4 minutes, then strain through a strainer and cool.

3 Gently melt the butter and sugar until dissolved. Pour into a bowl and cool for 2 minutes, then stir in the egg.

4 Sift the flour over the mixture and fold in. Blend the baking soda with the coffee-flavored milk and gradually stir into the mixture.

5 Pour into the pan, smooth the surface, and bake for 40 minutes, until well-risen and firm. Cool in the pan for about 10 minutes. Spoon the liqueur over the cake and set aside until cold. Loosen the edges with a metal spatula and turn out onto a wire rack.

6 To make the frosting, place the broken chocolate in a bowl over a pan of barely simmering water until melted. Remove from heat and stir in the butter and cream until smooth. Allow to cool before coating the top and sides of the cake, using a metal spatula. Let stand until set.

COFFEE ALMOND MARSALA CAKE

Roasted and crushed coffee beans are speckled throughout this delicious almond cake, distinctly flavored with Italian Marsala wine.

SERVES TEN TO TWELVE

INGREDIENTS
  ⅓ cup roasted coffee beans
  5 eggs, separated
  scant 1 cup sugar
  ½ cup Marsala wine
  6 tablespoons butter, melted
    and cooled
  1 cup ground almonds
  1 cup all-purpose flour, sifted
  ¼ cup chopped almonds
  confectioners' sugar, to dust
  crème fraîche, to serve

1 Preheat the oven to 350°F. Grease and line the bottom of a 9-inch springform pan with waxed paper. Put the coffee beans on a baking sheet and roast for about 10 minutes. Cool, then place in a large plastic bag and gently crush with a rolling pin.

2 In a large bowl, beat the yolks and generous ½ cup of the sugar until very pale in color and thick.

3 Stir in the crushed coffee, Marsala, butter and almonds. Sift the flour over, then carefully fold in.

4 Whisk the egg whites until they are stiff, then gradually incorporate the remaining sugar.

5 Fold into the almond mixture, a third at a time. Spoon into the pan and sprinkle the top with chopped almonds.

6 Bake for 10 minutes, then reduce the oven to 325°F and cook for another 40 minutes or until a skewer inserted into the center comes out clean. After 5 minutes, turn out and cool on a wire rack. Dust with confectioners' sugar and serve with crème fraîche.

SOUR CHERRY COFFEE LOAF

Dried sour cherries have a wonderfully concentrated fruit flavor and can be bought at supermarkets and health food stores.

SERVES EIGHT

INGREDIENTS
  12 tablespoons butter, softened
  scant 1 cup sugar
  1 teaspoon vanilla extract
  2 eggs, lightly beaten
  2 cups all-purpose flour
  ¼ teaspoon baking powder
  5 tablespoons strong brewed coffee
  1 cup dried sour cherries
For the frosting
  ½ cup confectioners' sugar, sifted
  ¼ cup strong brewed coffee

1 Preheat the oven to 350°F. Grease and line a 2-pound loaf pan with waxed paper. Cream the butter, sugar and vanilla until smooth.

2 Gradually add the eggs, beating well after each addition. Sift the flour and baking powder together.

3 Fold into the mixture with the coffee and ⅔ cup of the sour cherries. Spoon the mixture into the prepared pan and level the top.

4 Bake for 1¼ hours or until firm to the touch. Cool in the pan for 5 minutes, then turn out and cool on a wire rack.

5 To make the frosting, combine the confectioners' sugar, coffee and the remaining cherries. Spoon over the top and sides. Allow to set before slicing.

COFFEE AND MINT CREAM CAKE

GROUND ALMONDS GIVE THIS BUTTERY COFFEE CAKE A MOIST TEXTURE AND DELICATE FLAVOR. IT'S SANDWICHED TOGETHER WITH A GENEROUS FILLING OF CRÈME DE MENTHE BUTTERCREAM.

SERVES EIGHT

INGREDIENTS

   1 tablespoon ground coffee
   1½ tablespoons almost-boiling water
   12 tablespoons unsalted butter,
    softened
   scant 1 cup sugar
   2 cups self-rising flour, sifted
   ½ cup ground almonds
   3 eggs
   small sprigs of fresh mint,
    to decorate
For the filling
   4 tablespoons unsalted butter
   1 cup confectioners' sugar, sifted,
    plus extra for dusting
   2 tablespoons crème de
    menthe liqueur

1 Preheat the oven to 350°F. Lightly grease and line the bottoms of two 7-inch cake pans with waxed paper.

2 Put the coffee in a bowl and pour the hot water over. Allow to infuse for about 4 minutes, then strain through a strainer.

3 Put the butter, sugar, flour, almonds, eggs and coffee in a large bowl. Beat well for 1 minute, until blended. Divide the mixture evenly between the pans and level off. Bake for 25 minutes, until well-risen and firm to the touch. Let stand in the pans for 5 minutes, then turn out onto a wire rack to cool.

4 To make the filling, cream the unsalted butter, confectioners' sugar and crème de menthe liqueur together in a bowl until smooth.

COOK'S TIP
Make sure the butter is really soft and creamy before starting to mix the cake.

5 Remove the lining paper from the cake layers and sandwich together with the filling.

6 Generously dust the top with confectioners' sugar and place on a serving plate. Sprinkle with the fresh mint leaves just before serving.

COFFEE AND WALNUT JELLY ROLL WITH COINTREAU CREAM

COFFEE AND WALNUTS HAVE A NATURAL AFFINITY. HERE THEY APPEAR TOGETHER IN A LIGHT AND FLUFFY CAKE ENCLOSING A SMOOTH ORANGE CREAM.

SERVES SIX

INGREDIENTS
2 teaspoons ground coffee,
 e.g. mocha orange-flavored
1 tablespoon almost-boiling water
3 eggs
scant ½ cup sugar, plus extra
 for dusting
⅔ cup self-rising flour
½ cup toasted walnuts, finely
 chopped
For the Cointreau cream
generous ½ cup sugar
¼ cup cold water
2 egg yolks
8 tablespoons unsalted
 butter, softened
1 tablespoon Cointreau

1 Preheat the oven to 400°F. Grease and line a 13 x 9-inch jelly roll pan with baking parchment.

2 Put the coffee in a bowl and pour the hot water over. Allow to infuse for about 4 minutes, then strain through a strainer.

3 Whisk the eggs and sugar together in a large bowl until pale in color and thick. Sift the flour over the mixture and fold in with the coffee and walnuts. Turn into the pan and bake for 10–12 minutes, until springy to the touch.

4 Turn out on a piece of waxed paper sprinkled with sugar, peel off the lining paper and cool for about 2 minutes. Trim the edges, then roll up from one of the short ends, with the waxed paper where the filling will be. Allow to cool.

5 To make the filling, heat the sugar in the water over low heat until dissolved. Boil rapidly until the syrup reaches 220°F on a sugar thermometer. Pour the syrup over the egg yolks, whisking constantly, until thick and mousse-like. Gradually add the butter, then whisk in the orange liqueur. Allow to cool and thicken.

6 Unroll the cake and spread with the Cointreau cream. Re-roll and place on a serving plate seam-side down. Sprinkle with extra sugar and chill in the refrigerator until ready to serve.

COOK'S TIP
Decorate the roll with swirls of piped whipped cream and walnuts, if desired.

COFFEE CHOCOLATE MOUSSE CAKE

SERVE THIS DENSE, DARK CHOCOLATE CAKE IN SMALL PORTIONS, AS IT IS VERY RICH.

SERVES SIX

INGREDIENTS
  6 ounces semisweet chocolate
  2 tablespoons strong brewed coffee
  10 tablespoons butter, cubed
  ¼ cup sugar
  3 eggs
  ¼ cup ground almonds
  confectioners' sugar, for dusting
For the mascarpone and coffee cream
  generous 1 cup mascarpone
  2 tablespoons confectioners' sugar,
    sifted
  2 tablespoons strong brewed coffee

1 Preheat the oven to 400°F. Lightly grease and line the bottom of a 6-inch square pan with waxed paper.

2 Put the chocolate and coffee in a small heavy pan and heat over low heat until melted, stirring occasionally.

3 Add the butter and sugar to the pan and stir until dissolved. Whisk the eggs until frothy and stir into the chocolate mixture with the ground almonds.

4 Pour into the prepared pan, then put in a large roasting pan and pour in enough hot water to come two-thirds up the cake pan. Bake for 50 minutes or until the top feels springy to the touch. Allow to cool in the pan for 5 minutes, then turn the cake out upside-down on to a board and allow to cool.

5 Meanwhile, beat the mascarpone with the confectioners' sugar and coffee. Dust the cake generously with confectioners' sugar, then cut into slices. Serve on individual plates with the mascarpone and coffee cream.

COOK'S TIP
The top of this flourless cake, with its moist mousse-like texture, will crack slightly as it cooks.

CAPPUCCINO TORTE

THE FAMOUS AND MUCH LOVED BEVERAGE OF FRESHLY BREWED COFFEE, CREAMY MILK, CHOCOLATE AND CINNAMON IS TRANSFORMED INTO A SENSATIONAL DESSERT.

SERVES SIX TO EIGHT

INGREDIENTS
  6 tablespoons butter, melted
  10 ounces shortbread
    cookies, crushed
  ¼ teaspoon ground cinnamon
  1½ tablespoons powdered gelatin
  3 tablespoons cold water
  2 eggs, separated
  ½ cup light brown sugar
  4 ounces semisweet
    chocolate, chopped
  ¾ cup brewed espresso
  1⅔ cups whipping cream
  chocolate curls and ground
    cinnamon, to decorate

1 Mix the butter with the cookies and cinnamon. Spoon into the bottom of an 8-inch springform pan and press down well. Chill in the refrigerator while making the filling.

2 Sprinkle the gelatin over the cold water. Allow to soften for 5 minutes, then place the bowl over a pan of hot water and stir to dissolve.

3 Beat the egg yolks and sugar until thick. Put the chocolate in a bowl with the coffee and stir until melted. Add to the egg mixture, then cook gently in a pan for 1–2 minutes, until thickened. Stir in the gelatin. Set aside until just beginning to set, stirring occasionally.

4 Whip ⅔ cup of the cream until soft peaks form. Whisk the egg whites until stiff. Fold the cream into the coffee mixture, followed by the egg whites. Pour the mixture over the cookie crust and chill for 2 hours.

5 When ready to serve, remove the torte from the pan and transfer to a serving plate. Whip the remaining cream and place a dollop on top. Decorate with chocolate curls and a little cinnamon.

COFFEE-ORANGE CHEESECAKE

THIS RICH, COOKED AND CHILLED CHEESECAKE, FLAVORED WITH COFFEE AND ORANGE LIQUEUR, HAS A WONDERFULLY DENSE, VELVETY TEXTURE.

SERVES EIGHT

INGREDIENTS
   3 tablespoons almost-boiling water
   2 tablespoons ground coffee
   4 eggs
   generous 1 cup sugar
   2 cups cream cheese,
     at room temperature
   2 tablespoons orange liqueur,
     such as Curaçao
   ⅓ cup all-purpose flour, sifted
   1¼ cups whipping cream
   2 tablespoons confectioners' sugar,
     to dust
   light cream, to serve
For the base
   1 cup all-purpose flour
   1 teaspoon baking powder
   6 tablespoons butter
   ¼ cup sugar
   1 egg, lightly beaten
   2 tablespoons cold water

1 Preheat the oven to 325°F. Lightly grease and line an 8-inch springform pan with waxed paper.

2 Sift the flour and baking powder into a bowl. Rub in the butter until the mixture resembles fine bread crumbs. Stir in the sugar, then add the egg and water and mix to a dough. Press the mixture into the bottom of the pan.

3 To make the filling, pour the water over the coffee and allow to infuse for 4 minutes. Strain through a fine strainer.

4 Beat the eggs and sugar until thick. Using a wooden spoon, beat the cream cheese until softened, then beat in the liqueur, a spoonful at a time.

5 Gradually mix in the beaten eggs. Fold in the flour. Finally, stir in the whipping cream and coffee.

6 Pour the mixture over the crust and bake for 1½ hours. Turn off the heat and allow to cool in the oven with the door ajar. Chill the cheesecake in the refrigerator for 1 hour. Dust the top with the confectioners' sugar. Remove from the pan and place on a serving plate. Serve with light cream.

IRISH COFFEE CHEESECAKE

THE FLAVORS OF WHISKEY, COFFEE AND GINGER GO WELL TOGETHER, BUT YOU CAN VARY THE RECIPE BY USING GRAHAM CRACKERS FOR THE BASE OF THIS CHEESECAKE.

SERVES EIGHT

INGREDIENTS

3 tablespoons ground coffee
1 vanilla bean
1 cup light cream
1 tablespoon powdered gelatin
3 tablespoons cold water
2 cups cottage cheese, at room
   temperature
¼ cup Irish whiskey, such as
   Millars or Irish Velvet
½ cup light brown sugar
⅔ cup whipping cream
To decorate
⅔ cup whipping cream
chocolate-covered coffee beans
unsweetened cocoa powder,
   for dusting
For the base
5 ounces ginger cookies,
   finely crushed
¼ cup toasted almonds, chopped
6 tablespoons butter, melted

1 To make the base, mix together the crushed ginger cookies, toasted almonds and melted butter and press firmly into the bottom of an 8-inch springform pan. Chill in the refrigerator.

2 Heat the coffee, vanilla and light cream in a pan to the almost-boiling point. Cover and allow to infuse for 15 minutes. Strain through a fine strainer. Sprinkle the gelatin over the water in a bowl and let stand for 5 minutes. Place over a pan of simmering water until dissolved. Stir into the coffee cream.

3 Combine the cottage cheese, liqueur and sugar, then gradually blend in the coffee cream. Let stand until just beginning to set.

4 Beat the whipping cream until soft peaks form, and fold into the coffee mixture. Spoon into the pan and chill for 3 hours, until set.

5 To decorate, whisk the whipping cream until soft peaks form and spread lightly over the top. Chill for at least 30 minutes, then transfer to a serving plate. Decorate with chocolate-covered coffee beans and cocoa.

VARIATION

Instead of a smooth layer of cream on top of the cheesecake, pipe swirls of cream around the edge of the cake.

PIES, TARTS AND PASTRIES

The flavor and aroma of real coffee transforms perennial family favorites into something special, as you'll discover when you taste a slice of Coffee Custard Tart or Crunchy-Topped Coffee Meringue Pie. Along with these much-loved pies and tarts are classic pastries from around the world.

WALNUT PIE

SWEETENED WITH COFFEE-FLAVORED MAPLE SYRUP, THIS PIE HAS A RICH AND STICKY TEXTURE. THE WALNUTS CAN BE SUBSTITUTED WITH PECANS FOR A TRADITIONAL AMERICAN PIE.

SERVES EIGHT

INGREDIENTS
  2 tablespoons ground coffee
  ¾ cup maple syrup
  2 tablespoons butter, softened
  ¾ cup light brown sugar
  3 eggs, beaten
  1 teaspoon vanilla extract
  1 cup walnut halves
  crème fraîche or vanilla ice cream,
    to serve
For the pastry
  1¼ cups all-purpose flour
  pinch of salt
  ¼ cup confectioners' sugar
  6 tablespoons butter, cubed
  2 egg yolks

1 Preheat the oven to 400°F. To make the pastry, sift the flour, salt and confectioners' sugar into a bowl. Rub in the butter until the mixture resembles fine bread crumbs.

2 Add the egg yolks and mix into a dough. Turn out and knead on a lightly floured surface for a few seconds, until smooth. Wrap in plastic wrap and chill for 20 minutes.

3 Roll out the pastry and use to line an 8-inch fluted tart pan. Line with waxed paper and dried beans and bake for 10 minutes. Remove the paper and beans and bake for another 5 minutes. Take out the pastry shell and turn the oven to 350°F.

4 To make the filling, put the coffee and maple syrup in a small pan and heat until almost boiling. Remove from heat and let stand until just warm. Combine the butter and sugar, then gradually beat in the eggs. Strain the maple syrup mixture through a fine strainer into the bowl and stir in with the vanilla extract.

5 Arrange the walnuts in the pastry shell, then carefully pour in the filling. Bake for 30–35 minutes or until lightly browned and firm. Serve warm with crème fraîche or vanilla ice cream.

MISSISSIPPI MUD PIE

THIS LONG-TIME FAVORITE WAS NAMED AFTER THE MUDDY BANKS OF THE MISSISSIPPI RIVER. THIS VARIATION HAS A DENSE LAYER OF CHOCOLATE MOUSSE, TOPPED WITH A COFFEE TOFFEE LAYER AND, FLOATING ON TOP, LOTS OF FRESHLY WHIPPED CREAM.

SERVES EIGHT

INGREDIENTS
For the crust
    10 ounces graham crackers, crushed
    10 tablespoons butter, melted
For the chocolate layer
    2 teaspoons powdered gelatin
    2 tablespoons cold water
    6 ounces semisweet chocolate,
      broken into squares
    2 eggs, separated
    ⅔ cup heavy cream
For the coffee toffee layer
    2 tablespoons ground coffee
    1¼ cups heavy cream
    1 cup sugar
    4 tablespoons cornstarch
    2 eggs, beaten
    1 tablespoon butter
    ⅔ cup whipping cream and chocolate
      curls, to decorate

1 Grease an 8½-inch springform pan. Mix together the graham cracker crumbs and butter and press into the bottom and sides of the pan. Chill for 30 minutes.

2 To make the chocolate layer, sprinkle the gelatin over the cold water and let stand for 5 minutes. Put the bowl over a pan of hot water and stir until dissolved. Melt the chocolate in a bowl over hot water. Stir in the gelatin.

3 Blend the egg yolks and cream and stir into the chocolate. Whisk the egg whites and fold into the mixture. Pour into the pie shell and chill for 2 hours.

4 To make the coffee layer, put the coffee in a bowl. Reserve 4 tablespoons of cream. Heat the remaining cream to almost-boiling and pour over. Allow to infuse for 4 minutes. Strain through a strainer back into the pan. Add the sugar and heat gently until dissolved.

5 Mix the cornstarch with the reserved cream and the eggs. Add to the coffee and cream mixture and simmer gently for 2–3 minutes, stirring.

6 Stir in the butter and allow to cool for 30 minutes, stirring occasionally. Spoon over the chocolate layer. Chill in the refrigerator for 2 hours.

7 To make the topping, whip the cream until soft peaks form and spread thickly over the coffee toffee layer. Decorate with chocolate curls and chill until ready to serve.

CRUNCHY-TOPPED COFFEE MERINGUE PIE

A SWEET PASTRY SHELL IS FILLED WITH A COFFEE CUSTARD AND A MERINGUE TOPPING—CRUNCHY AND GOLDEN ON THE OUTSIDE AND SOFT AND "MARSHMALLOWY" UNDERNEATH.

SERVES SIX TO EIGHT

INGREDIENTS

For the pastry
  1½ cups all-purpose flour
  1 tablespoon confectioners' sugar
  6 tablespoons butter
  1 egg yolk
  finely grated zest of ½ orange
  1 tablespoon orange juice

For the filling
  2 tablespoons ground coffee
  1½ cups milk
  4 tablespoons cornstarch
  ½ cup sugar
  4 egg yolks
  1 tablespoon butter

For the meringue
  3 egg whites
  ¼ teaspoon cream of tartar
  ¾ cup superfine sugar
  ¼ cup peeled hazelnuts
  1 tablespoon light brown sugar

1 Preheat the oven to 400°F. Sift the flour and confectioners' sugar into a bowl. Rub in the butter until the mixture resembles bread crumbs. Add the egg yolk, orange zest and juice and mix into a firm dough. Wrap in plastic wrap and chill for 20 minutes. Roll out and use to line a 9-inch loose-bottomed fluted tart pan. Cover with plastic wrap and chill for 30 minutes.

COOK'S TIP
The pastry shell can be made up to 36 hours in advance, but once filled and baked the pie should be eaten on the day of making.

2 Prick the pastry all over, line with waxed paper and dried beans and bake for 15 minutes, removing the paper and beans for the last 5 minutes. Turn the oven to 325°F.

3 To make the filling, put the coffee in a bowl. Heat 1 cup of the milk until almost-boiling and pour over the coffee. Allow to infuse for 4 minutes, then strain. Blend the cornstarch and sugar with the remaining milk in a pan and whisk in the coffee-flavored milk.

4 Bring the mixture to a boil, stirring until thickened. Remove from heat.

5 Beat the egg yolks. Stir in a little of the hot coffee mixture into the egg yolks, then add to the remaining coffee mixture with the butter. Cook the filling over low heat for 3–4 minutes, until very thick. Pour into the pastry shell.

6 To make the meringue, whisk the egg whites and cream of tartar until stiff. Whisk in the superfine sugar, a spoonful at a time.

7 Spoon the meringue over the filling and spread right to the edge of the pastry, swirling into peaks. Sprinkle with hazelnuts and light brown sugar and bake for 30–35 minutes or until golden brown and crisp. Serve warm, or cool on a wire rack and serve cold.

COFFEE CUSTARD TART

A SCRUMPTIOUS WALNUT PASTRY SHELL, FLAVORED WITH VANILLA, IS FILLED WITH A SMOOTH CREAMY COFFEE CUSTARD, BAKED UNTIL LIGHTLY SET AND TOPPED WITH CREAM.

SERVES SIX TO EIGHT

INGREDIENTS
1 vanilla bean
2 tablespoons ground coffee
1¼ cups light cream
⅔ cup milk
2 eggs, plus 2 egg yolks
¼ cup sugar
confectioners' sugar, for dusting
lightly whipped heavy cream, to serve

For the pastry
1½ cups all-purpose flour
2 tablespoons confectioners' sugar
8 tablespoons butter, cubed
½ cup walnuts, finely chopped
1 egg yolk
1 teaspoon vanilla extract
2 teaspoons ice water

1 Preheat the oven to 400°F. Put a baking sheet in the oven. Sift the flour and sugar into a bowl. Rub in the butter until the mixture resembles bread crumbs. Stir in the walnuts. Mix together the egg yolk, vanilla extract and water. Add to the dry ingredients and mix into a dough. Wrap in plastic wrap and chill for 20 minutes.

2 Roll out the dough and use to line a deep plain or an 8-inch fluted tart pan, using a knife to smooth the edges. Chill again for 20 minutes. Prick the shell with a fork. Fill with waxed paper and dried beans and bake on the hot baking sheet for 10 minutes. Remove the paper and beans and bake for another 10 minutes. Turn the oven to 300°F.

3 Split the vanilla bean and scrape out the seeds. Put both in a pan with the coffee, cream and milk. Heat until almost-boiling, cover and infuse for 10 minutes. Remove the vanilla bean pod. Whisk the eggs, egg yolks and sugar together.

4 Bring the cream back to boiling point and pour onto the egg mixture, stirring. Strain into the pastry shell.

5 Bake the tart for 40–45 minutes or until lightly set. Take out of the oven and set on a wire rack to cool. Remove the tart from the pan, pipe cream rosettes around the edge and dust with confectioners' sugar to serve.

BLUEBERRY FRANGIPANE FLAN

A TANGY LEMON PASTRY SHELL IS FILLED WITH A SWEET ALMOND FILLING DOTTED WITH RIPE BLUEBERRIES. THE JAM AND LIQUEUR GLAZE ADDS AN INDULGENT FINISH.

SERVES SIX

INGREDIENTS
    2 tablespoons ground coffee
    3 tablespoons almost-boiling milk
    4 tablespoons unsalted butter
    ¼ cup sugar
    1 egg
    1 cup ground almonds
    1 tablespoon all-purpose flour, sifted
    2 cups blueberries
    2 tablespoons seedless
      blackberry jam
    1 tablespoon liqueur, such as
      Amaretto or Cointreau
    mascarpone, crème fraîche or
      sour cream, to serve
For the pastry
    1½ cups all-purpose flour
    8 tablespoons unsalted butter
    2 tablespoons sugar
    finely grated zest of ½ lemon
    1 tablespoon ice water

1 Preheat the oven to 375°F. Sift the flour into a bowl and rub in the butter. Stir in the sugar and lemon zest, then add the water and mix to a firm dough. Wrap in plastic wrap and chill for 20 minutes.

2 Roll out the pastry on a lightly floured surface and use to line a 9-inch loose-bottomed fluted tart pan. Line the pastry with waxed paper and dried beans and bake for 10 minutes. Remove the paper and beans and bake for another 10 minutes. Remove from the oven.

3 Meanwhile, to make the filling, put the coffee in a bowl. Pour the milk over and allow to infuse for 4 minutes. Cream the butter and sugar until smooth. Beat in the egg, then add the almonds and flour. Strain in the coffee through a fine strainer and fold in.

COOK'S TIP

This flan can also be made in individual tartlets. Use six 4-inch tartlet pans and bake for 25 minutes.

4 Spoon the coffee mixture into the pastry shell and spread evenly. Sprinkle the blueberries over the top and push them down slightly into the mixture. Bake for 30 minutes, until firm, covering with tinfoil after 20 minutes.

5 Remove from the oven and allow to cool slightly. Heat the jam and liqueur in a small pan until melted. Brush over the flan and remove from the pan. Serve warm with a scoop of mascarpone or with crème fraîche or sour cream.

TIA MARIA TRUFFLE TARTS

THE IDEAL DESSERT FOR A TEA OR COFFEE BREAK, THESE MINI COFFEE PASTRY SHELLS ARE FILLED WITH A CHOCOLATE LIQUEUR TRUFFLE CENTER AND TOPPED WITH FRESH RIPE BERRIES.

SERVES SIX

INGREDIENTS

   1¼ cups heavy cream
   generous ¾ cup seedless blackberry
     or raspberry jam
   5 ounces semisweet chocolate,
     broken into squares
   3 tablespoons Tia Maria liqueur
   1 pound mixed berries, such as
     raspberries, small strawberries
     or blackberries
For the pastry
   2 cups all-purpose flour
   1 tablespoon sugar
   10 tablespoons butter, cubed
   1 egg yolk
   2 tablespoons very strong brewed
     coffee, chilled

1 Preheat the oven to 400°F. Put a baking sheet in the oven to heat. To make the pastry, sift the flour and sugar into a large bowl. Rub in the butter. Stir the egg yolk and coffee together, add to the bowl and mix to a stiff dough. Knead lightly on a floured surface for a few seconds until smooth. Wrap in plastic wrap and chill for about 20 minutes.

2 Use the pastry to line six 4-inch fluted tartlet pans. Prick the bases with a fork and line with waxed paper and dried beans. Put on a hot baking sheet and bake for 10 minutes. Remove paper and beans and bake for 8–10 minutes longer, until cooked. Cool on a wire rack.

3 To make the filling, slowly bring the cream and a generous ½ cup of the jam to a boil, stirring constantly until dissolved.

COOK'S TIP
When making the pastry, blend the egg yolk and coffee together until thoroughly combined to get an evenly colored pastry.

4 Remove from heat, add the chocolate and 2 tablespoons of the liqueur. Stir until melted. Cool, then spoon into the pastry shells, and smooth the tops. Chill for 40 minutes.

5 Heat the remaining jam and liqueur until smoothly blended. Arrange the fruit on top of the tarts, then brush the jam glaze over it. Chill until ready to serve.

COFFEE CREAM PROFITEROLES

DELICIOUS COFFEE CHOUX PASTRY PUFFS ARE FILLED WITH CREAM AND DRIZZLED WITH A WHITE CHOCOLATE SAUCE. FOR THOSE WITH A SWEET TOOTH, THERE IS PLENTY OF EXTRA SAUCE.

SERVES SIX

INGREDIENTS
   9 tablespoons all-purpose flour
   pinch of salt
   4 tablespoons butter
   ⅔ cup brewed coffee
   2 eggs, lightly beaten
For the white chocolate sauce
   ¼ cup sugar
   scant ½ cup water
   5 ounces good quality white dessert
      chocolate, broken into pieces
   2 tablespoons unsalted butter
   3 tablespoons heavy cream
   2 tablespoons coffee liqueur, such
      as Tia Maria or Kahlúa
To assemble
   1 cup heavy cream

1 Preheat the oven to 425°F. Sift the flour and salt onto a piece of waxed paper. Cut the butter into pieces and put in a pan with the coffee.

2 Bring to a rolling boil, then remove from heat and add all the flour. Beat until the mixture leaves the sides of the pan. Allow to cool for 2 minutes.

3 Gradually add the eggs, beating well between each addition. Spoon the mixture into a pastry bag fitted with a ½-inch plain nozzle.

4 Pipe about 24 small cream puffs onto a dampened baking sheet. Bake for 20 minutes, until well risen.

5 Remove the puffs from the oven and pierce the side of each with a sharp knife to let out the steam.

6 To make the sauce, put the sugar and water in a heavy pan and heat gently until dissolved. Bring to a boil and simmer for 3 minutes. Remove from heat. Add the chocolate and butter, stirring until smooth. Stir in the cream and liqueur.

7 To assemble, whip the cream until soft peaks form. Using a pastry bag, fill the choux puffs through the slits in the sides. Arrange on plates and pour a little of the sauce over, either warm or at room temperature. Serve the remaining sauce separately.

DANISH COFFEE PASTRIES

THESE WORLD-FAMOUS PASTRIES ARE TIME-CONSUMING TO MAKE, BUT WELL WORTH THE EFFORT.

MAKES SIXTEEN

INGREDIENTS
3 tablespoons almost-boiling water
2 tablespoons ground coffee
generous ½ cup sugar
3 tablespoons unsalted butter
1 egg yolk
1 cup ground almonds
beaten egg, to glaze
1 cup apricot jam
2 tablespoons water
1½ cups confectioners' sugar
½ cup chopped almonds, toasted
¼ cup candied cherries
For the pastry
2½ cups all-purpose flour
¼ teaspoon salt
1 tablespoon sugar
1 cup butter, softened
2 teaspoons active dry yeast
1 egg, beaten
scant ½ cup cold water

1 Sift the flour, salt and sugar into a bowl. Rub in 2 tablespoons butter. Stir in the yeast. Stir the egg and water, add to the bowl and mix to a soft dough. Lightly knead for 4–5 minutes. Put in a plastic bag and chill for 15 minutes.

2 Put the remaining butter between 2 sheets of waxed paper and pound with a rolling pin to make a 7-inch square. Roll out the dough to about a 10-inch square. Put the butter in the middle, like a diamond, then bring up each corner of dough to fully enclose it.

3 Roll out the pastry to about 14 inches long. Turn up the bottom third of the pastry, then fold down the top third. Seal the edges together with a rolling pin. Return the pastry to the plastic bag and chill for 15 minutes.

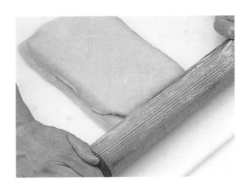

4 Repeat the rolling and folding three more times, each time turning the pastry so that the short ends are at the top and bottom. Allow a 15-minute rest between each turn.

5 To make the filling, pour the hot water over the coffee and infuse for 4 minutes. Strain through a fine strainer. Cream the sugar and butter together. Beat in the egg yolk, ground almonds and 1 tablespoon of the coffee.

6 Divide the dough and filling equally into three. Roll one dough portion to a 7 x 14-inch rectangle. Spread with filling and roll up from a short end. Cut into six equal slices. Roll another portion into a 10-inch square; cut into a 10-inch round, remove the trimmings and cut into six segments.

7 Put a spoonful of filling at the widest end of each triangle, then roll up towards the point into a crescent.

8 Roll out the remaining dough into an 8-inch square; cut into fourths. Put some filling into the center of each. Make cuts from each corner almost to the center and fold four alternate points to the center.

9 Preheat the oven to 425°F. Put the pastries on greased baking sheets, spaced apart. Cover loosely with oiled plastic wrap and leave to rise for 20 minutes, until almost doubled in size. Brush with beaten egg and bake for 15–20 minutes, until lightly browned and crisp. Cool on wire racks.

10 Put the jam in a pan with the water; bring to a boil, then strain. Brush the jam over the warm pastries. Mix the confectioners' sugar with the remaining coffee, adding more water if necessary to make a thick icing. Drizzle the icing over some of the pastries and decorate some with almonds or chopped candied cherries. Allow to set before serving.

GREEK FRUIT AND NUT PASTRIES

AROMATIC SWEET PASTRY CRESCENTS, KNOWN AS "MOSKHOPOUNGIA" IN GREECE, ARE PACKED WITH CANDIED CITRUS PEEL AND WALNUTS, SOAKED IN A COFFEE SYRUP.

MAKES SIXTEEN

INGREDIENTS
  ¼ cup honey
  ¼ cup strong brewed coffee
  ½ cup mixed candied citrus peel,
    finely chopped
  1 cup walnuts, chopped
  ¼ teaspoon freshly grated nutmeg
  milk, to glaze
  superfine sugar, for sprinkling
For the pastry
  4 cups all-purpose flour
  ½ teaspoon ground cinnamon
  ½ teaspoon baking powder
  pinch of salt
  10 tablespoons unsalted butter
  2 tablespoons sugar
  1 egg
  ½ cup chilled milk

1 Preheat the oven to 350°F. To make the pastry, sift the flour, ground cinnamon, baking powder and salt into a bowl. Rub in the butter until the mixture resembles fine bread crumbs. Stir in the sugar. Make a well in the middle.

2 Beat the egg and milk together and add to the well in the dry ingredients. Mix to a soft dough. Divide the dough into two and wrap each in plastic wrap. Chill in the refrigerator for 30 minutes.

3 Meanwhile, to make the filling, mix the honey and coffee. Add the peel, walnuts and nutmeg. Stir well, cover and allow to soak for at least 20 minutes.

4 Roll out a portion of dough on a lightly floured surface until about ⅛-in thick. Stamp out rounds using a 4-inch round cutter.

5 Place a heaping teaspoonful of filling on one side of each round. Brush the edges with a little milk, then fold over and press the edges together to seal. Repeat with remaining pastry until all the filling is used.

6 Put the pastries on lightly greased baking sheets, brush with milk and sprinkle with superfine sugar.

7 Make a steam hole in each with a skewer. Bake for 35 minutes or until lightly browned. Cool on a wire rack.

BAKLAVA

Turkish coffee is black, thick, very sweet and often spiced. Here it is used in this famous pastry confection, traditionally served on religious festival days in Turkey.

MAKES SIXTEEN

INGREDIENTS
½ cup blanched almonds, chopped
½ cup pistachios, chopped
scant ½ cup sugar
4 ounces phyllo pastry
6 tablespoons unsalted butter,
   melted and cooled
For the syrup
generous ½ cup sugar
3-inch piece cinnamon stick
1 whole clove
2 cardamom pods, crushed
5 tablespoons strong brewed coffee

1 Preheat the oven to 350°F. Combine the nuts and sugar. Cut the pastry to fit a pan measuring 7 x 11 inches. Brush the pan with a little butter. Lay a sheet of pastry in the pan and brush with melted butter.

2 Repeat with three more sheets and spread with half the nut mixture.

3 Layer on three more sheets of pastry, lightly brushing butter between the layers, then spread the remaining nut mixture over them, smoothing it over the entire surface. Top with the remaining pastry and butter. Gently press down the edges to seal.

4 With a sharp knife, mark the top into diamonds. Bake for 20–25 minutes, until golden brown and crisp. Meanwhile, put the syrup ingredients in a small pan and heat gently until the sugar has dissolved. Cover with a lid and let sit for 20 minutes.

5 Remove the baklava from the oven. Reheat the syrup and strain over the pastry. Allow to cool in the pan. Cut into diamonds, remove from the pan and serve.

COOK'S TIP
While assembling the baklava, keep the pile of phyllo pastry covered with a damp cloth to keep it from getting brittle, which makes it difficult to use.

CANDIES, COOKIES AND BREADS

Few people can resist the tantalizing display of cookies and breads in a bakery window, but it's easy to recreate those delectable treats at home. Here, you'll find a selection of traditional and unusual recipes, from rich and gooey truffles to a stunning candied fruit braid.

STUFFED PRUNES

CHOCOLATE-COVERED PRUNES, SOAKED IN LIQUEUR, HIDE A MELT-IN-YOUR-MOUTH COFFEE FILLING.

MAKES APPROXIMATELY THIRTY

INGREDIENTS
    1 cup pitted prunes
    ¼ cup Armagnac
    2 tablespoons ground coffee
    ⅔ cup heavy cream
    12 ounces semisweet chocolate,
      broken into squares
    ½ tablespoon vegetable shortening
    2 tablespoons unsweetened cocoa
      powder, for dusting

1 Put the pitted prunes in a bowl and pour the Armagnac over. Stir, then cover with plastic wrap and set aside for 2 hours or until the prunes have absorbed the liquid.

COOK'S TIP
Fresh dates can be used instead of prunes, if preferred.

2 Make a slit along each prune to remove the pit, making a hollow for the filling, but leaving the fruit intact.

3 Put the coffee and cream in a pan and heat to almost-boiling. Cover, infuse for 4 minutes, then heat again until almost-boiling. Put 4 ounces of the chocolate into a bowl and pour over the coffee cream through a strainer.

4 Stir until the chocolate has melted and the mixture is smooth. Allow to cool, until it has the consistency of softened butter.

5 Fill a pastry bag with a small plain nozzle with the chocolate mixture. Pipe into the cavities of the prunes. Chill in the refrigerator for 20 minutes.

6 Melt the remaining chocolate in a bowl over a pan of hot water. Using a fork, dip the prunes one at a time into the chocolate to give them a generous coating. Place on baking parchment to harden. Dust each with a little of the cocoa powder.

COFFEE CHOCOLATE TRUFFLES

BECAUSE THESE CLASSIC CHOCOLATES CONTAIN FRESH CREAM, THEY SHOULD BE STORED IN THE REFRIGERATOR AND EATEN WITHIN A FEW DAYS.

MAKES TWENTY-FOUR

INGREDIENTS
12 ounces semisweet chocolate
5 tablespoons heavy cream
2 tablespoons coffee liqueur, such as Tia Maria or Kahlúa
4 ounces good quality white dessert chocolate
4 ounces good quality milk dessert chocolate

1 Melt 8 ounces of the semisweet chocolate in a bowl over a pan of barely simmering water. Stir in the cream and liqueur, then chill the mixture in the refrigerator for 4 hours, until firm.

2 Divide the mixture into 24 equal pieces and quickly roll each into a ball. Chill for one more hour, or until they are firm again.

3 Melt the remaining semisweet, white and milk chocolate in separate small bowls. Using two forks, carefully dip eight of the truffles, one at a time, into the melted milk chocolate.

4 Repeat with the white and plain chocolate. Place the truffles on a board, covered with waxed paper or tinfoil. Allow to set before removing and placing in a serving bowl or individual paper liners.

VARIATIONS
Make variations by adding one of the following to the truffle mixture:
Ginger—Stir in ¼ cup finely chopped crystallized ginger.
Candied fruit—Stir in ⅓ cup finely chopped candied fruit, such as pineapple and orange.
Pistachio—Stir in ¼ cup, chopped peeled pistachios.
Hazelnut—Roll each ball of chilled truffle mixture around a whole peeled hazelnut.
Raisin—Soak generous ¼ cup raisins overnight in 1 tablespoon coffee liqueur, such as Tia Maria or Kahlúa, and stir into the truffle mixture.

CHOCOLATE AND COFFEE MINT THINS

THESE COFFEE-FLAVORED CHOCOLATE SQUARES CONTAIN PIECES OF CRISPY MINTY CARAMEL AND ARE IDEAL FOR SERVING WITH AFTER-DINNER COFFEE.

MAKES SIXTEEN

INGREDIENTS
scant ½ cup sugar
5 tablespoons water
3 drops oil of peppermint
1 tablespoon strong-flavored
    ground coffee
5 tablespoons almost-boiling
    heavy cream
8 ounces semisweet chocolate
½ tablespoon unsalted butter

COOK'S TIP
Don't put the chocolate in the refrigerator to set, or it may lose its glossy appearance and become too brittle to cut easily into neat squares.

1 Line a 7-inch square pan with baking parchment. Gently heat the sugar and water in a heavy pan until dissolved. Add the peppermint, and boil until a light caramel color.

2 Pour the caramel onto an oiled baking sheet and allow to harden, then crush into small pieces.

3 Put the coffee in a small bowl and pour the hot cream over. Allow to infuse for about 4 minutes, then strain through a fine strainer. Melt the chocolate and unsalted butter in a bowl over barely simmering water. Remove from heat and beat in the hot coffee cream. Stir in the mint caramel.

4 Pour the mixture into the prepared pan and smooth the surface level. Set aside in a cool place to set for at least 4 hours, preferably overnight.

5 Carefully turn out the chocolate onto a board and peel off the lining paper. Cut the chocolate into squares with a sharp knife and store in an airtight container until needed.

COFFEE AND HAZELNUT MACAROONS

MACAROONS ARE TRADITIONALLY MADE WITH GROUND ALMONDS. THIS RECIPE USES HAZELNUTS, WHICH ARE LIGHTLY ROASTED BEFORE GRINDING, BUT YOU CAN USE WALNUTS INSTEAD, IF PREFERRED.

MAKES TWENTY

INGREDIENTS
edible rice paper
⅔ cup peeled hazelnuts
generous 1 cup sugar
1 tablespoon ground rice
2 teaspoons ground coffee,
    e.g. hazelnut-flavored
2 egg whites
superfine sugar, for sprinkling

1 Preheat the oven to 350°F. Line two baking sheets with rice paper. Place the peeled hazelnuts on another baking sheet and cook for 5 minutes. Cool, then place in a food processor and grind until fine.

2 Mix the ground nuts with the sugar, ground rice and coffee. Stir in the egg whites to make a fairly stiff paste.

3 Spoon into a piping bag fitted with a ½-inch plain nozzle. Pipe rounds on the rice paper, allowing room to spread.

4 Sprinkle each macaroon with a little superfine sugar, then bake for 20 minutes or until pale golden in color. Transfer to a wire rack to cool. Remove excess rice paper when completely cold. Serve immediately or store in an airtight container for up to 2–3 days.

COFFEE AND MACADAMIA MUFFINS

THESE MUFFINS ARE DELICIOUS EATEN COLD, BUT ARE BEST SERVED STILL WARM FROM THE OVEN.

MAKES TWELVE

INGREDIENTS
    1½ tablespoons ground coffee
    1 cup milk
    4 tablespoons butter
    2½ cups all-purpose flour
    2 teaspoons baking powder
    10 tablespoons light brown sugar
    ½ cup macadamia nuts
    1 egg, lightly beaten

1 Preheat the oven to 400°F. Lightly grease a 12-cup muffin or a popover pan with oil. Alternatively, line with paper muffin liners.

2 Put the coffee in a large cup or bowl. Heat the milk to almost-boiling and pour it over. Allow to infuse for 4 minutes, then strain through a strainer.

3 Add the butter to the coffee-flavored milk mixture and stir until melted. Let stand until cold.

4 Sift the flour and baking powder into a large mixing bowl. Stir in the sugar and macadamia nuts. Add the egg to the coffee-flavored milk mixture, pour into the dry ingredients and stir until just combined—do not over-mix.

5 Divide the coffee mixture between the prepared muffin pan and bake for about 15 minutes, until well risen and firm. Transfer to a wire rack and serve warm or cold.

COOK'S TIP
To cool the coffee-flavored milk quickly, place the cup in a large bowl of ice or cold water.

CHUNKY WHITE CHOCOLATE AND COFFEE BROWNIES

BROWNIES SHOULD HAVE A MOIST AND CHEWY TEXTURE, SO TAKE CARE NOT TO OVERCOOK THEM— WHEN READY, THE MIXTURE WILL BE SLIGHTLY SOFT UNDER THE CRUST, BUT WILL FIRM AS IT COOLS.

MAKES TWELVE

INGREDIENTS
    1½ tablespoons ground coffee
    3 tablespoons almost-boiling water
    11 ounces semisweet chocolate,
      broken into pieces
    1 cup butter
    1 cup sugar
    3 eggs
    ⅔ cup self-rising flour, sifted
    8 ounces white chocolate, chopped

1 Preheat the oven to 375°F. Grease and line the bottom of a 7 x 11-inch pan with waxed paper. Put the coffee in a bowl and pour the water over. Allow to infuse for 4 minutes, then strain through a strainer.

2 Put the semisweet chocolate and butter in a bowl over a pan of hot water and stir occasionally until melted. Remove from heat and cool for 5 minutes.

3 Combine the sugar and eggs. Stir in the chocolate and butter mixture and the coffee. Stir in the sifted flour.

4 Fold in the white chocolate pieces. Pour into the prepared pan.

5 Bake for 45–50 minutes or until firm and the top is crusty. Allow to cool in the pan. When completely cold, cut into squares and remove from the pan.

PECAN TOFFEE SHORTBREAD

COFFEE SHORTBREAD IS TOPPED WITH PECAN-STUDDED TOFFEE. CORNSTARCH GIVES IT A CRUMBLY LIGHT TEXTURE, BUT ALL ALL-PURPOSE FLOUR CAN BE USED, TOO.

MAKES TWENTY

INGREDIENTS
   1 tablespoon ground coffee
   1 tablespoon almost-boiling water
   8 tablespoons butter, softened
   2 tablespoons smooth peanut butter
   scant ½ cup sugar
   ⅔ cup cornstarch
   1⅔ cups all-purpose flour
For the topping
   12 tablespoons butter
   ¾ cup light brown sugar
   2 tablespoons light corn syrup
   1 cup shelled pecans,
     coarsely chopped

1 Preheat the oven to 350°F. Lightly grease and line the bottom of a 7 x 11-inch pan with waxed paper.

2 Put the ground coffee in a small bowl and pour the hot water over. Allow to infuse for 4 minutes, then strain through a fine strainer.

3 Cream the butter, peanut butter, sugar and coffee together until smooth. Sift the cornstarch and flour together and mix in to make a smooth dough.

4 Press into the bottom of the pan and prick all over with a fork. Bake for 20 minutes. To make the topping, put the butter, sugar and syrup in a pan and heat until melted. Bring to a boil.

5 Allow to simmer for 5 minutes, then stir in the chopped nuts. Spread the topping over the shortbread. Let stand in the pan until cold, then cut into fingers. Remove from the pan and serve.

COFFEE BISCOTTI

THESE CRUNCHY COOKIES ARE MADE TWICE AS DELICIOUS WITH BOTH FRESHLY ROASTED GROUND COFFEE BEANS AND STRONG AROMATIC BREWED COFFEE IN THE MIXTURE.

MAKES ABOUT THIRTY

INGREDIENTS

⅓ cup espresso-roasted coffee beans
⅔ cup blanched almonds
scant 2 cups all-purpose flour
1½ teaspoons baking powder
¼ teaspoon salt
6 tablespoons unsalted butter, cubed
¾ cup sugar
2 eggs, beaten
1½–2 tablespoons strong
  brewed coffee
1 teaspoon ground cinnamon,
  for dusting

1 Preheat the oven to 350°F. Put the espresso coffee beans in a single layer on one side of a large baking sheet and the almonds on the other. Roast for 10 minutes. Allow to cool.

2 Put the coffee beans in a blender or food processor and process until fairly fine. Turn out and set aside. Process the almonds until finely ground.

3 Sift the flour, baking powder and salt into a bowl. Rub in the butter until the mixture resembles fine bread crumbs. Stir in the sugar, ground coffee and almonds. Add the beaten eggs and enough brewed coffee to make a fairly firm dough.

COOK'S TIP
Store the biscotti in an airtight container for at least a day before serving.

4 Lightly knead for a few seconds until smooth and shape into two rolls about 3 inches in diameter. Place on a greased baking sheet and dust with cinnamon. Bake for 20 minutes.

5 While still hot, cut the rolls using a sharp knife into 1½-inch slices on the diagonal. Arrange the slices on the baking sheet and bake for another 10 minutes or until lightly browned. Cool on a rack.

CAPPUCCINO PANETTONE

THIS LIGHT BREAD IS SERVED IN ITALY AS PART OF THEIR CHRISTMAS FARE. IT'S TRADITIONALLY A TALL LOAF WITH A DOME ON THE TOP, FORMED BY THE RICH YEAST DOUGH AS IT RISES.

SERVES EIGHT

INGREDIENTS
  4 cups all-purpose flour
  ½ teaspoon salt
  scant ½ cup sugar
  ¼-ounce envelope active dry yeast
  8 tablespoons butter
  scant ½ cup very hot strong brewed
    espresso coffee
  ½ cup milk
  4 egg yolks
  ⅔ cup semisweet chocolate chips
  beaten egg, to glaze

1 Preheat the oven to 375°F. Lightly grease and line a deep 5½–6-inch cake pan with waxed paper. Sift the flour and salt into a large bowl. Stir in the sugar and yeast.

2 Add the butter to the coffee and stir until melted. Stir in the milk, then add to the dry ingredients with the egg yolks. Combine to make a dough.

COOK'S TIP
Unlike commercial varieties, homemade panettone should be eaten within a day or two of baking.

3 Turn the dough out onto a lightly floured surface and knead for 10 minutes, until smooth and elastic. Knead in the chocolate chips.

4 Shape into a ball, place in the pan and cover with oiled plastic wrap. Allow to rise in a warm place for 1 hour or until the dough reaches the top of the pan. Lightly brush with beaten egg and bake for 35 minutes.

5 Turn down the oven to 350°F and cover the panettone with tinfoil if it has browned enough. Cook for another 10–15 minutes or until done.

6 Allow the panettone to cool in the pan for 10 minutes, then transfer to a wire rack. Remove the lining paper just before slicing and serving.

CANDIED FRUIT BREAD

THE CENTER OF THIS COFFEE-FLAVORED YEASTED BRAID CONTAINS BRIGHTLY COLORED CANDIED FRUITS, MOISTENED BY SOAKING IN RICH COFFEE LIQUEUR.

SERVES SIX TO EIGHT

INGREDIENTS

   1 cup mixed candied fruit, such as
      pineapple, orange and cherries,
      chopped
   ¼ cup coffee liqueur, such as Tia
      Maria or Kahlúa
   2 tablespoons ground coffee
   ½ cup almost-boiling milk
   2 cups all-purpose flour
   ¼ teaspoon salt
   2 tablespoons light brown sugar
   ¼-ounce envelope active dry yeast
   1 egg, beaten
   2 ounces white almond paste, grated
   ¼ cup apricot jam
   1 tablespoon unsalted butter
   1 tablespoon sugar
   1 tablespoon honey

1 Put the candied fruit in a small bowl and spoon the coffee liqueur over. Stir to coat the fruit, then cover with plastic wrap and allow to soak overnight.

2 Preheat the oven to 400°F. Put the coffee in a bowl; pour the hot milk over and let stand until tepid. Strain through a fine strainer. Sift the flour and salt into a bowl. Stir in the brown sugar and yeast. Make a well in the center, add the coffee-flavored milk and the egg and mix to a soft dough.

3 Knead for 10 minutes. Put the dough in a clean bowl, cover with plastic wrap and allow to rise for 1 hour.

4 Meanwhile, combine the soaked fruit, almond paste and jam. Lightly knead the dough again for 1 minute, then roll out to a rectangle 14 x 12 inches.

5 Spread the filling in a 3-inch strip lengthwise down the middle to within 2 inches of each end. Make 14 diagonal cuts about ¾-inch wide in the dough on either side of the filling.

6 Fold the ends of the dough up over the filling, overlapping alternate strips, Tuck in the last two strips neatly. Place on a greased baking sheet.

7 Cover with plastic wrap and allow to rise for 20 minutes. Melt the butter, sugar and honey in a small pan, then brush over the braid. Bake for 20–25 minutes. Allow to cool before slicing and serving.

INDEX

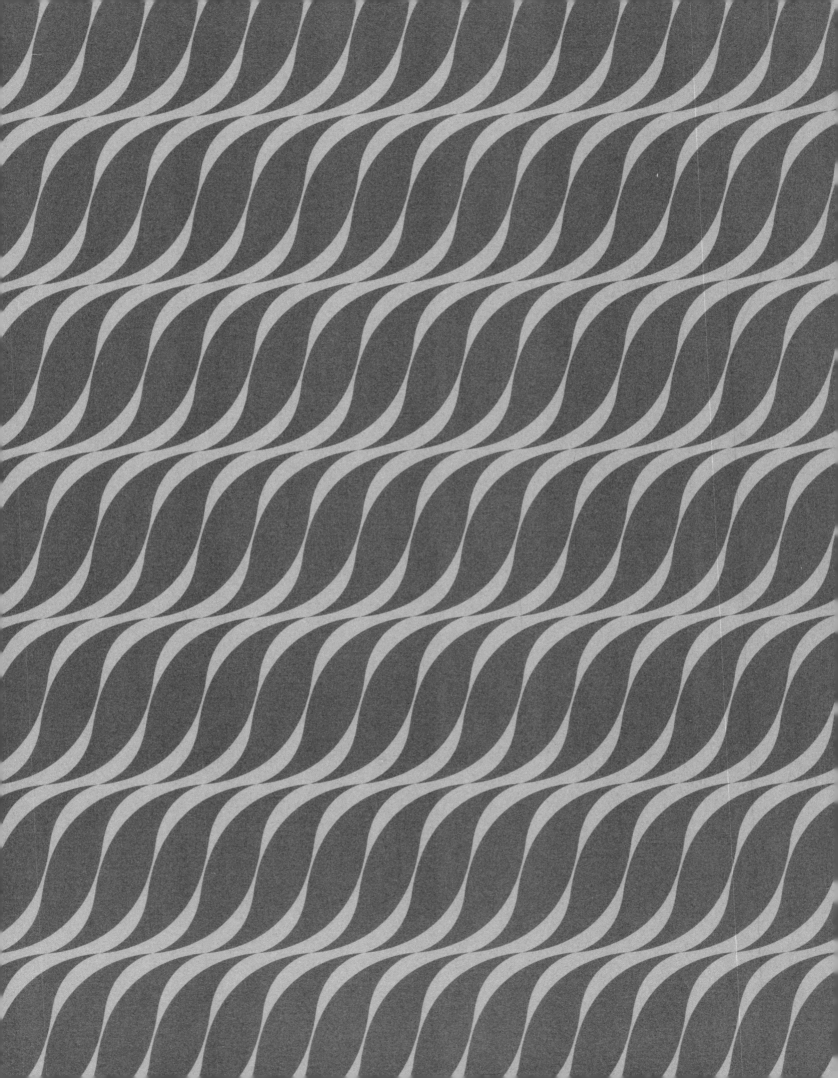